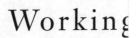Working

WORKING *North*
DEW Line to Drill Ship

RICK RANSON

NEWEST PRESS

National Library of Canada Cataloguing in Publication Data
Ranson, Rick, 1949-
Working north: DEW line to drill ship / Rick Ranson.

ISBN 1-896300-73-1

1. Ranson, Rick, 1949- 2. Canada, Northern—Biography. I. Title.
FC3963.1.R36A3 2003   971.9'03'092   C2003-910947-X

Editor for the Press: Ross Jopling
Copy editor: Carol Berger
Cover and interior design: Ruth Linka
Cover photo: CANMAR
Interior photos: All photos were taken by the author except for:
Page 36, Polar Bear by Jocyline Lariviere
Page 132, Grain Elevator in Churchill by Vincent K. Chan, www.arcticcircle.ca
Maps: Wendy Johnson, Johnson Cartographics
Author photograph: Image2, Winnipeg, Manitoba

NeWest Press acknowledges the support of the Canada Council for the Arts, the Alberta Foundation for the Arts, and the Edmonton Arts Council for our publishing program. We also acknowledge the financial support of the Government of Canada through the Book Publishing Industry Development Program (BPIDP) for our publishing activities.

NeWest Press
201–8540–109 Street
Edmonton, Alberta T6G 1E6
(780) 432-9427
www.newestpress.com

1   2   3   4   5   06   05   04   03

PRINTED AND BOUND IN CANADA

For Sheila, Rebecca, Tara, and Jessie,
the girls I left behind.

Contents

The DEW Line site at Cape Dyer on Baffin Island. I always took the dogs along when I went for a walk—they would occupy any polar bear looking for a snack.

I was the only one awake when we flew through the northern lights. It was two in the morning. Winnipeg was a couple of hours behind me and Hall Beach, my destination, was over an hour away. Except for the quiet hiss of the 737's cabin, everything was still. Slowly the night sky, the faces of the sleeping passengers, and the pages of the book I was reading all turned an imperial purple. I held my hand up to the light, then turned my gaze back to the window. Shades of purple danced across the entire sky. I looked around to see if anyone else was watching—they were all fast asleep. An hour later, the sky faded to black.

The Arctic captures you. The most striking thing is the light. It's different up there. In high summer the sun skips across the horizon, picking up every colour in the spectrum. On a winter's night, although darkness covers everything, the sky sparkles with glinting frost crystals and the stars above.

Money was the big attraction. Back in the eighties, when most of these stories took place, I was banking a thousand dollars every week—after taxes and expenses. I paid off my house in eight years. With the money that was made, a lot of men started businesses. Some started farms, several others bought rental properties. And some, after thirty years in the business, lived in boarding houses with only a mortgaged pick-up truck and beer money to their name. It was a profound environment to work in. Beauty, grandeur, danger, boredom, cold, life, death, beer.

I was first hired as a boilermaker because every DEW site had a powerhouse with boilers. Once hired, I mentioned that I also had my journeyman's certificate as a welder. My supervisors then gave me a double classification—boilermaker and welder. If there were no boilers to fix, I would repair and fabricate construction and road equipment, which the other employees seemed to use in demolition derbies. Because I was flexible, my problem was not so much getting in, it was getting out. There was always work for a handyman.

The stories in this book are grouped into two sections. The first section describes my experiences on the DEW Line. I started there in 1983 and left around 1987. Shortly after, I started to work for oil companies on their drill ships and construction sites. That period makes up the second half of the book. Geographically, all the stories take place on a rough line along the Arctic Circle, from Cape Dyer on Baffin Island to Prudhoe Bay, Alaska.

During my time up north I sent letters to my family, some describing events that appear in this book. A few years ago I decided to turn one of those letters into a story. I sent it off to a magazine that published it and gave me $175.00. I took a creative writing course for $165.00 and started working on some of the other letters. This book is the result. All the stories are true, or based on actual events. I'm fond of telling my wife, "You know me, honey, I have never, ever, ever, ever exaggerated in my life."

For publication, I have changed some identities, with notable exceptions: Brian Crow, the sailor who saved my ass, now a captain of a cargo ship sailing out of Vancouver; Bob Sanderson, my boilermaker buddy; Darryl McLaughlin, the cook who outran a polar bear, still a cook, still working the north; Al Shell, my old welder friend, found frozen in his car in a snowstorm.

Years after moving south, I still think of the Arctic with affection and longing. In the north, the whites are stark, the land is acid-washed, and the air is clean. Life is simple there. But for all its beauty, it has a mean streak. If you're careful and resourceful, you get to live another day. If you're foolish or just unlucky, it can kill you faster than a lightning strike. Danger was part of the attraction—up there, I had more interesting things happen in one day than an entire month in the city. I'd go back in a heartbeat.

Arctic Ocean

ELLESMERE

ISLAND

Alert

Nanisivik

Davis Strait

Clyde River

VICTORIA
ISLAND

M'Clintock Channel

BAFFIN

Cape Hooper

Broughton I

Cape
Dyer

Cambridge Bay

Cape Felix

ISLAND

Gjoa Haven

Hall
Beach

JENNY LIND I.

Arctic Circle

Foxe
Basin

Iqaluit

NUNAVUT

NORTHWEST
TERRITORIES

Hudson
Bay

QUEBEC

SASKATCHEWAN

MANITOBA

ONTARIO

0   250 km

PART ONE
DEW LINE

DEW Line site at Cape Hooper.
Once there were twenty-one DEW sites. Now there's only a couple or so manned sites and a lot of computers. Back before the dead eyes of vigilant, silent satellites, each small, isolated site was manned by a dozen or so very human technicians.

I knew the DEW Line was going to be a very different place to work at the first union meeting. When the rep asked if there were any comments or grievances from the membership, you didn't have to be a student of human nature to see that something was bothering the radar technician. Jittery eyes and twitching limbs pretty much gave away any surprise attack from Red. With an intense display of indignation he demanded it be put on record that the company was negligent. Negligent because those coffee creamers they supplied were made with palm oil. Palm oil caused cancer. A study had been done. On rats. Although it concluded you could only get cancer if you consumed thirty gallons of pure palm oil a day for over ten years, Red was adamant. Not only was the company negligent, "they" probably knew about "it" all along.

"Been up here long, buddy?"

I gathered, by the bulging-eyed, spittle-punctuated response, that yes indeed, he had been up here waaaay too long. From then on we made sure we weren't caught alone with Red.

The Distant Early Warning (DEW) Line is a series of radar

stations spanning Canada's north, just above the Arctic Circle. Each station, separated by a hundred miles of tundra, was built in the 1950s by the Pentagon, with Canada tagging along. It would watch for the great hordes of Russian bombers and intercontinental missiles that were sure to come. It's impressive just how fast it was conceived, built, shipped, assembled, manned, and operated. The Russians built their own version soon after. In the fifties, it was good to be paranoid.

At one time there were radar sites all over the north. The Alert station was the northernmost in Canada. Then came the DEW Line, the Pine Tree Line, and finally the Mid-Canada Line. There were lines strung out all around the world. Beginning in Hawaii, DEW hop-scotched off ships turning lazy circles in the North Pacific. Arriving on the Alaska Peninsula, it followed the Aleutian mountain range into Canada, then on to Greenland, Iceland, and western Europe. It was our way of telling the Russians "Don't make a move pardner, we got ya surrounded." I hope they were impressed. It sure cost a lot.

Each site had a huge umbrella of radar that overlapped its neighbours—a built-in safety should an individual station go down. A typical DEW site looked like a very long white mobile home on stilts. One long building on the outside, and one long hallway on the inside. People slept at one end and worked at the other. In the middle we met, ate, watched TV, and drank. A white geodesic dome rose above the structure, covering a huge, fly swatter-shaped radar antenna. It revolved at a constant pace, so that if you were watching videos in the lounge, every minute or so the TV would emit this annoying little *meeeep*. Another dose of microwaves blowing through your body.

When it's –45 Celcius (or Fahrenheit, for that matter), people don't much open their windows. The air inside the station smelled like yesterday's socks. The janitorial staff fought a good fight, but was destined to lose. Forty years of sweat and other bodily fluids, bleach, musty furniture, and dead skin beat them back. Years later, people who have lived even for a short time on a site can instantly recall the smell.

The food on the DEW Line was basic and plentiful. The cooks had a lot of power and could make or break the morale of an entire station. Of all the years I travelled on the DEW Line, only once did I encounter a bad cook. He often served the same dish three times a day, with the excuse that the supply plane had been delayed and there was simply no other food. This was perfectly understandable, but it was the only excuse he ever used, and we knew better. The station chief, for some unknown reason, turned a deaf ear to all complaints—until most of his staff requested transfers to other sites. Then he had to answer to his bosses why nobody wanted to work on his site. The cook left shortly after that. Surprisingly, the supply plane didn't come for several days after the new cook arrived, but the food improved immediately.

At first, the DEW Line was operated exclusively by the military. Over the years, however, the day-to-day operations were handed over to civilians. The routine remained as structured and systematic as before, but a definite civilian attitude prevailed.

To get from the power house, where we worked, to the kitchen, you had to go through the radar room, which contained all the top-secret electronic equipment. While the blue uniforms from the Pentagon were on base, anyone who was hungry, but not "authorized" to see that room, had to leave the building, trudge through the snow and wind, and go around to the back door. The moment the military left that site, the station chief called me and my partner into his office. He asked us if we were spies.

"No, for pete's sake. I'm from Winnipeg and Sanderson's from Portage." I told him.

"No I'm not. I'm from Sanford." said Bob.

"OK, well, I'm going to open up the radar room so you guys can cut through. You've been tracking mud through the hallway. Just don't look at anything."

We happily took the shortcut for the rest of our tour. It turned out to be a big disappointment because the really secret stuff was in another room. I never got up the nerve to tell them I was actually from Transcona.

The DEW Line was just normal men and women doing a boring job in a boring place that they couldn't easily leave. Even the money was irrelevant. It was deposited directly into your bank account down south. I once left home for a rotation with fifty dollars in my pocket. Three months later I came home with thirty-five. My wife wanted to know what I blew the fifteen bucks on.

What everyone who worked up there remembers most is the stories. The funny, pathetic, adventurous, or just plain odd stories that make people human. There's the story of the sheet-metal worker who was repairing equipment out past the airstrip. Our luckless tin man was too far away from the site when nature called. A little while later, nature demanded. With the −30 degree, razor-sharp arctic wind whipping around his nether regions, he squatted and prepared to pollute. He was so concerned about the freezing of certain valuable parts of his anatomy that he didn't notice that in the wind the hood of his parka had flopped back and was making a receptacle for his deposit. When he stood and put up his hood, he noticed.

There's the story of the Great Peregrine Falcon Drop. Some DEW Line employees found a dead falcon, and nearby, its nest. In that nest was one lone, half-starved baby falcon. So the group adopted the baby and fed it around the clock. They nursed it back to health. They made a cage for it and gave it scraps of meat from the table. It got quite large. Chubby might be the correct word. Over the next weeks, the falcon lost its baby fuzz and got its wings. Every day it grew bigger. It was constantly exercising its wings, flapping around the warehouse, bouncing up and down, wanting to take off. It wanted to fly, to be free! One Sunday morning, bright and early, the entire off-duty personnel on the site gathered at the base of the radio tower, camcorders and pre-focused cameras at the ready. With the falcon tucked into his jacket, the radio technician climbed to the top of the tower. Once on top, he shouted at us all to get set. He held the bird in his hand and opened his palm to the world. The bird flapped its wings, hopped out of the outstretched palm and exercised its freedom. Two hundred and four feet, didn't open a wing.

An exciting story happened to one guy, and unfortunately for him, it was recorded on film. The picture was handed around from site to site with the caption "You know you're an idiot when your last words are *Hey everybody, watch this!*" A bear had fallen asleep in the bright spring sunlight. He just happened to doze near a radar site. The DEW Liners went out to take pictures of the warm and fuzzy. Now, a sleeping polar bear is a very appealing animal. It's creamy-white, round, fluffy, and soft. But what most southerners don't realize is that a polar bear is a creamy-white, round, fluffy, soft serial killer. Every time it wants to eat, it kills something. Most seals don't die of old age. They don't die of arthritis. They don't die of cancer and they don't die of heart disease. They die when a polar bear eats them. It doesn't discriminate between seal meat and people meat. Meat's meat, and when someone gets too close, the bear's reaction can be summed up in one word—buffet!

The DEW Liners stood by the truck in the bright sunlight and took several pictures. Our luckless hero didn't have a telescopic lens and wanted to get a little closer. So, ignoring the low warnings of his companions, who remained by the safety of the truck, he edged closer. There was no reaction from the bear. Emboldened by the lack of response, the photographer edged closer. More comments came from the companions. The edger edged some more. The companions cocked their cameras, because their buddy was now well past the safety zone. All of a sudden, the bear started to take an interest in this moveable feast.

There's a moment in every fool's life when he knows that he's pushed a little too far. Usually it's his last. The bear stood up and decided that although he didn't order it, it had been delivered anyway, so he might as well eat it.

When confronted by a polar bear, you are to remain calm. You should discard some outer clothing to distract it. You are to face it, and slowly back away, retreating to a safe place. Whatever your situation, never ever turn your back on a polar bear.

Screaming, abject terror splashed across his face, polar bear right on his sorry ass, the DEW Liner ran all the way back to the truck. He would have made a sprinter on steroids envious. *Click, click, click* went the cameras of his friends. *Click, click, click,* went his promising career on the DEW Line.

There's the story of the worker who went to take a shower. Wrapped in his robe, with towel and soap at the ready, he found the shower running, so he waited his turn. He waited, and then waited some more. Finally, he asked the person behind the shower screen to hurry up. No answer. Strange, because he could hear the *burp, burp, burp* of movement coming from within. After several minutes, good manners gone, he gingerly spread the curtain and peeked into the stall. Naked as a jaybird, luxuriating in the longest, freshest, coldest shower in her happy young life was a baby seal. Round, black eyes, innocent and unconcerned, looked up at the robed intruder as if to say "Do you mind? I'm taking a shower!"

Once, there were twenty-one DEW sites. Now there are only a couple or so manned sites and a lot of computers. Back before the dead eyes of vigilant, silent satellites, each small, isolated site was manned by a dozen or so very human technicians. These technicians watched their green-lit radar scopes and listened to electronic crackle in their headphones. They waited for an enemy that never came. Like a modern-day version of the Pony Express, the DEW Line served its purpose and then, overtaken by a greater technology, it died.

The real enemy that each and every DEW Liner fought was boredom, the slow cancer of tedium that spread over and suffocated the unwary.

A hundred years from now visitors will come upon an installation in the high Arctic that's covered in snow and ice. They'll walk along the side of the long, white building and stare, transfixed by the huge dome above the main structure. They'll see the small outbuildings, the scrap iron, and what's left of the dead equipment, lined up neatly for yet another inspection.

"What did they do here, what was its purpose?" They will wonder. To that, I must answer that for a brief while, we stood on guard for thee, using the only equipment we had, the best there was. Like ancient guards in a lonely outpost on the Great Wall of China, or Hadrian's Wall, we watched, we waited, and we slowly went nuts.

The major stood apart from the crew as his suitcases were hastily unloaded from the small, silver airplane. Avoiding the questioning looks, he surveyed his new domain. Where he stood was so far north that Russia was closer than the United States. He was as far away from civilization as possible without leaving the planet.

He had been banished to the radar site, his career in shreds, because of a barking dog. Unfortunately, he had lived beside that dog. Day in and day out, the bloody thing had barked. It started when its owner left for work at 7:00 AM and stopped when he returned at 5:00 PM. No amount of friendly hints could convince the owner that there was a problem. Faced with this indifference, the major hatched a plan. He fed the dog a sweet, powerful laxative through the fence every afternoon, just before 5:00. The dog never caught onto the theory of cause and effect, and within weeks both he and his master's carpets were gone. The major's only mistake was getting drunk and telling a friend, who told a friend, who told a friend, who told someone who was not a friend, who told the neighbour, who was a general. The major got his own lesson in cause and effect.

DEPARTMENT OF DEFENCE PRODUCTION

WARNING

THE OFFICIAL SECRETS ACT

CHAPTER 49, STATUTES OF CANADA, 1939
as amended

IT IS AN OFFENCE PUNISHABLE BY
IMPRISONMENT UP TO 14 YEARS

1. To inspect, enter, make or obtain a sketch of, any military, naval or air force establishment or factory or place used for the manufacture of munitions or defence supplies, for any purpose prejudicial to the safety or interests of the State or which might be useful to a foreign power.

2. To disclose any code word, password, sketch, plan, model or information to any person other than a person authorized or to whom it is a duty in the interest of the State to communicate it.

3. To keep any official plans, specifications, models, documents or codes without lawful authority.

4. To disclose or deliver any such plans, specifications, models, documents or codes to unauthorized persons or to fail to take reasonable care of them.

TAKE NOTICE THAT THE FOREGOING IS
ONLY A BRIEF SUMMARY OF PART OF

THE OFFICIAL SECRETS ACT

Date of Issue
February, 1952

Deputy Minister.

Once unloaded from the airplane that was for him and him alone, the major was bundled with the rest of the baggage into a military truck, which proceeded to thump up the hill. The site, part of the DEW Line, sat alone on a bleak, white ocean of snow. It was on a direct line between somewhere and nowhere. The technicians who kept the machinery humming spent their days in a world of cryptic codes, green-tinted screens, weather forecasts, half-lit rooms, and the metallic crackle of far-away voices. Their off-hours were spent in the bar, staring vacantly at their drinks, or staring vacantly at videos, or staring vacantly at well-worn magazines. It was as if they stood alone outside in the cold, with their noses pressed against the world's window. They spent their lives sitting, watching, and waiting, never able to participate. The crew of that DEW site dreamed of action, any action. They would get drunk on Saturday night so they could have roaring hangovers on Sunday. Sunday morning hangovers gave them something to do.

The site had a bar that was a converted bedroom. In it, four men could have a conversation or a game of cards. Five was a crowd. The room was full of overstuffed chairs, touching each other in a semi-circle. They smelled of forty years of stale popcorn, spilled drinks, and sitting men. If some junior capitalist wanted to gather some loose change by reaching down between the cushions, he did it only once.

Sitting in the bar were three friends. One American and two Canadians. Or was it the other way around? It didn't matter whose country belonged to whom, they suffered equally from the boredom. They grumbled at their lot in life. They grumbled about their wives, or their lack thereof. They talked about the NFL, the CFL, the NHL, the NBA, and the SBL (stupid brother-in-law). They talked about why they came north and they talked about what they would do when they headed back south. They drank too much cheap liquor and told amazing stories that were stuck to the truth with an elastic band. They enjoyed themselves in the slow easy fashion of good friends, comfortable with each other on a lazy Sunday afternoon. It was to be the last slice of the peaceful times for a long while.

In front of the radar site, standing on either side of the gravel road, were two rusted flagpoles topped by two worn and tattered flags. Flapping in the constant arctic winds, the flags had lost their colour, their shape, and a third of their size. Bumping along in the truck, the major winced as he passed them. He was the only military man posted to the site. Until he had arrived, there were a dozen civilians split evenly between Americans and Canadians. Together for years, these men had formed either friendships or hates. The isolation of the place had created a few cases of questionable sanity. The civilians on that radar site need not have worried about the major's sanity. He was already mad.

He saw what he considered lethargy and sloth, and with the same creative quirk that got him there, decided to shape everyone up by starting a war. The phone lines hummed and a monstrous c-130 Hercules airplane landed the following week. Off came a huge, gleaming, stainless-steel flagpole. Sun glinted and danced along its entire phallic length. Men stopped their daily routine to come down to the airstrip to see the latest addition to the site. Huskies sniffed the new object and stared at the crowd, wondering what all the fuss was about. The first shot of the war had been fired.

The new commanding officer's plan started to work. The Canadians gathered and straggled out to the scrap pile where rusted pipe was kept. Days later, an equally long, gleaming, schedule-40 galvanized pipe rose across the road to match its American neighbour. Once the pole was erected, the Canadians standing around it broke into an impromptu rendition of *O Canada*. The Americans present clapped and cheered along with the Canadians. The mood was shattered by an enthusiastic American, caught up in the first genuine excitement he had had in months, yelling out . . .

"Now let's all sing it in French!"

There was a long pause while the small group of Canadians looked searchingly at each other, studying the clouds, the snow on the ground. Padded feet shuffled in the crunchy snow.

"Ah, fight fair, Yank."

"Yeah, fight fair. Jeez, that's a dirty trick."

"Yeah, no fair. That's low."

The Americans, who honestly thought that every Canadian could sing the national anthem in both official languages, were instantly ashamed of having committed a major international incident. So, the small group of contrite Americans bought the small group of Canadians all the Budweisers and Molsons they could drink, smug in the knowledge that they, at least, knew the words to their own national anthem. They just had problems keeping within shouting distance of the tune. Long into the night they talked about the NFL, the CFL, the NBA, the NHL, and Pamela Anderson.

"She's ours!"

"She's ours!"

"Screw you, she's MINE!"

War is hell.

The major diverted another airplane and a huge duffel bag

arrived at the landing strip. Next morning, the sun rose on the biggest Old Glory that anyone had ever seen outside of the backdrop of George C. Scott acting in the movie *Patton*. Both Canadians and Americans walked around the flag in awe. The gleaming, polished pole quivered under the weight of the flag flapping majestically in the arctic wind.

"Holy cow," said the Canadians.

"Shoot," said the Americans.

"You white guys are all crazy," said the Inuit.

That night the Canadians held a council of war in the bar. The Americans were definitely not invited, unless of course they bought beer. The bar was packed. Long into the night schemes and dreams were advanced, recorded, rejected. Slowly, a beery plan materialized. It seemed that one of the Canadians had a brother-in-law. This brother-in-law had two advantages: one, he was a waiter at one of those restaurants that had a huge flag in the front, and two, he was just crazy enough to steal it. In due course, aboard the weekly supply plane a huge burlap bag arrived addressed to the relative who now had to find his brother-in-law a new job.

The next morning, two of the largest flags north of the Arctic Circle snapped in the wind, their poles humming under the weight. A small group of Americans and Canadians gathered to admire the spectacle.

"Hey, wasn't that restaurant owned by Americans?"

"Yeah, but so's my member of parliament."

"Ah."

That evening, the bar was packed. In one of the few awkward moments of the war, one of the Canadians wrote a message on the notice board. In bold letters was written ZINCU WINDA WAR YANKEE DOG? The other Canadians quickly admonished him and apologized profusely to the Americans, most of whom were still trying to figure it out. Chastened, the culprit mumbled that he had only repeated what he had heard in a John Wayne movie. The embarrassed Canadians bought the Americans beer and they talked about the NBA, the NFL, the CFL, the NHL and Michael J. Fox.

"He's ours!"

"He's ours!"

"Screw you, he's . . ."

"How long you been up here, buddy?"

An hour later, one of the Americans looked at the now blank notice board. As enlightenment slowly spread across his face, he shouted, "Hey!"

The Canadians quickly bought him another beer. On cue, the other Americans all shouted, "Hey!"

The Canadians bought them all beer. Clever people, those Yanks.

Events quickly escalated. The major commandeered the portable lighting plant. When the sun went down that night the diesel generator was fired up. In a spectacular blaze, Old Glory received several million candlepower of brittle blue-white light from the station's searchlight. Framed by the vast, black arctic night, the flag shone, its reds, blues, and whites flashed and snapped in the wind. Bathed in the light from below, the brilliant colours lit the surrounding snow for miles around. As the generator thumped, and the pole quivered under the weight, the ropes *ting-ting-tinged* against the pole, as the Americans stood as one, and lovingly watched their flag. A couple of off-duty Canadians thudded their mittened hands and cheered their friends. The Americans turned, and through the frost and darkness you could see the white of smiling teeth. Then they all went back to the bar and toasted each other's country. Military jets flying at twenty thousand feet could plainly see the illuminated flag.

The Canadians held another council of war in the bar, followed by a quick trip to the stores department. Without the aid of wires, radar waves passing through a fluorescent light bulb will illuminate it. If someone stands close enough to a radar tower holding a fluorescent light, that tube will flash like magic in his hands. The Canadians proceeded to hang fluorescent tubes up and down their flagpole. The next night, beside the brilliantly lit American flag, was an arctic Las Vegas. Every time the radar antenna rotated within the white walls of its dome, the Canadian flagpole would flash. Ghostly white in the inky black night, the Red, White and Red slowly undulated and flowed in a slow-motion strobe-light dance. The Canadians, not normally given to patriotic display, watched the symbol of their country with moist eyes, shuffling their mukluks in the crunchy snow, hoping nobody else would notice. The Americans hung back for a while, then let loose with spontaneous cheering and clapping. Then everybody went back to the bar and toasted each other's country.

Boredom was a thing of the past. Parties and secret conferences that turned out to be parties were ongoing. Meetings in the hallway spilled over into the bar and then back out into the snow. The crew hadn't had so much fun since the summer supply ship had arrived with a woman onboard—and no one could figure out which one she was.

At night, European-bound airplanes, flying six miles high, could distinctly pick up a blazing American flag, and right beside it, a flashing Canadian monster. The flag war became the topic of gossip all along the DEW Line. The crews

A C-130 Hercules on the tarmac. This was often used by the US Air Force to deliver cargo to the various DEW sites.

of commercial airliners brought news of the site south and a military plane on a routine mission diverted to take pictures of the flags. Unknown to the combatants on the radar site, however, the war and its parties, laughter, and camaraderie would soon come to an abrupt halt.

Generals are a very impressive breed of human. Their uniforms do not wrinkle. People make way for them. They walk into a room with the same effect as a battleship in an ocean full of canoes. When the army puts stars on their shoulders, generals lose all traces of humour. This particular general showed up in his own plane, inspected the flags, and left. Fifteen minutes later, the American flag was down and stored in the hangar. Gone was the generator with its powerful lights. In its place stood a regulation flag and a regulation flagpole. The Americans on the site looked longingly at where their beautiful flag had whip-cracked in the arctic wind just the night before.

Although they were not ordered to, the Canadians took down their monster flag and stored it in the hangar beside the other bundle. They hunted around in the scrap pipe storage and found a steel pole that was close to regulation. Quietly, they dug out their old tattered flag and hung it beside the regulation American flag. The war was over.

In place of the Great Flag War was a vast, sucking vacuum of boredom. Mind-numbing, desperate boredom, intertwined with tedium and a dash of loneliness. Men who had laughed and clapped each other on the back weeks before barely spoke when passing in the halls. Off duty, people sat, nursed their beer, stared out the windows, and waited for the months to inch by until it was their "plane day."

Days, weeks, then months dragged on. A new season started. Crackling cold and white turned to fog, mist, and mosquitoes. Months after the war, two Americans and one Canadian, (or was it the other way around?) sat making slow, bored conversation in the bar. They spoke of the war like a long gone but fondly remembered football game. There was a long pause as the Canadian studied the lines in his American friend's face. It was as if he was trying to decide something rather important.

"What?" the impatient friend demanded.

With a slow smile across his face, the Canadian leaned towards the American and purposefully betrayed his country. "You know how we felt pretty bad about you having to stop the fun so we made our flag the same as yours?"

"Yeah," was the hesitant reply.

"Well, we didn't. Not quite."

The Americans stared at him intently.

"Well, you know how the General ordered you to make the new flagpole regulation size? We made ours an inch taller than yours."

The Americans exploded.

"Get the flagpole out of the hangar! Where's the flag? Get the searchlight! You Redcoats are sneaky bastards! You haven't heard the last of us! Buy us a beer, you rat! Buy us lots!"

Later that evening, a small, rather unsteady group of figures could be seen down by the American flagpole placing a one-inch block under the flag's base. Or was it two inches?

Looking inland from the Cape Hooper DEW site. One of the Alaskan adventurers sets out with his dog team on a bid to circumnavigate Baffin Island.

Cape Hooper is located on the east coast of Baffin Island. Surrounded by precipitous cliffs that rise from the beach, it is almost inaccessible to the rest of humanity. The landing strip, where planes bearing the names of Canadian mammals land and take off, is situated on the beach. A black hangar sits alone, a square in a sea of jumbled rocks. Its purpose is not to store aircraft, but runway maintenance equipment. Airplanes do not stay on the ground for very long.

Lining the strip were forty-five-gallon drums filled with rocks. Each held a white and orange barber pole with a blue light on top. The lights started from the hangar at the seaward end of the airstrip and ended at the base of the cliff. As a plane landed, the pilot had a long time to look into the silent, deadly rocks straight ahead.

Etched into the mountain was a road of sorts. With an upward angle that broke most highway codes, and with more flicks than a sperm's tail, the road switchbacked its way up the 2,000 feet to the radar site. It approached the top at such an angle that from the last switchback, a traveller had the impression of arriving from almost underneath.

A set of military-issue outbuildings housed the supplies

and protected the equipment. The main white-slate building stood alone at the pinnacle of Cape Hooper. The long, narrow structure housed radar and weather equipment that cost more to get it there than it was now worth, a set of diesel generators, a couple of offices, kitchen, lounge, bar, and bedrooms. I've seen bigger airplanes.

Cape Hooper is sterile. Warm it isn't. It could freeze the bolts off a snowmobile. From the Davis Strait side, where ice squeaks and rumbles against itself, the Cape looks like a loaf of rye bread, rising 2,000 feet straight up from the ice prairie. With its great stone hunchback to the sea, landward Cape Hooper is sliced on a gentle slope towards the plains below. It would be a great place for a seaport. The cape, like a gigantic prow of a ship, protects the beach from the gales of the arctic sea.

From the water, the radar site looked like a Greek monastery, sitting high atop the cliffs. From the valley, it looked like a Tibetan castle. Passing Inuit hunters once told us that they could see our lights like lighthouse beacons as far as thirty miles up the night-blackened coast.

The DEW Line, by and large, is a straight line. Most of the sites were settled roughly parallel to, and just above, the Arctic Circle. All except Cape Hooper, which sat out like a sore thumb, well up the Baffin Island coast. It was an easy site to miss, even for the weekly scheduled flights.

Working so alone and isolated from civilization, DEW Liners became quite sensitive to territory. The overwhelming silence soon pervaded all areas of life. Loud conversation was suspect. Loud noise was prohibited. After several months, it was difficult to avoid the pull of that soft, fluffy silence.

The workers carried their space like a bubble around

themselves. Come too close and there would be a reaction in proportion to the length of time they had been isolated. Madness was not uncommon. Depression was universal. The military had devised a simple but effective method to avoid these problems. Work! Keep them occupied. Dig a hole and then fill it up! Don't think. Obey! Check the machinery! Tick off the jobs done! Round the bases, and touch each one, and touch them exactly in the way we want them touched. Miss a tick on a sheet and we'll show you how much it matters. Work, work, woooork!

Lounging in the tiny bar, blankly watching the latest batch of videos, two off-duty DEW Liners put hours behind them waiting for their eventual return to the world. A door slammed with a resounding thud. This was very odd because they were the only off-duty people on the site. It was also odd that it came from the back door, which was never used, unless a fire or a polar bear was chomping on someone's ass. The sound of boots thumped down the hall. Boots were not allowed inside the building. In unison, two heads turned, watched, and waited. In lumbered two abominable snowmen, a seven-foot high blur of black and brown ragged fur.

"Evening," the first fur spoke.

"Evening," the second fur spoke.

With an odd grace and purpose, the two figures continued on through the room and exited the other side. TV forgotten, the two heads followed the furs like synchronized cuckoo clocks.

"Gotta be American."

"Yeah, no Canadian is nuts enough to come up here, unless they have to."

"Yeah, they know what they're gettin' themselves into."

"Yeah."

"Yeah."

The two Canadians ran down the hall after the abominable Americans.

They were from Red Dog, Alaska, a place so small it wasn't on the Rand McNally in the office. In the summer they were commercial fishermen, part-time mountain guides, and full-time adventurers. They had kayaked Cape Horn, climbed the Himalayas, and watched friends die guiding in the mountains of Alaska. They had talked about trying the Iditarod.

Their current adventure was to dogsled around Baffin Island. The plan was to start at Iqaluit and travel on the ice up the coast north to Nanasivik, then back south to finish where they had started. They had planned to live off the land, feeding themselves and the dogs by hunting seal along the way. Unfortunately, the seal were several hundred miles out in the middle of Davis Strait. The fish were close, but they might as well have been as far away as the seals because they were under six to ten feet of ice. The DEW Liners had seen hungry animals before, but they had never seen people this hungry. They had spent the last week living off their spit. A dog had died. The surviving huskies had that lean and hungry look. Attempt to pet them and lose your hand.

The abominable one with light-brown hair didn't want his picture taken. The smaller one was more amiable. Both had frostbite sores to their faces and fingers. Between the two of them they shared maybe a pound of fat. In T-shirts, they looked like greyhounds compared to our several layers of fat brought on by idleness. The cook took them under his wing and tried to fatten them up in the short time they were with us.

The trip had been planned from far-off Alaska. They had flown to Iqaluit with dogs, gear, and the encouragement of all their friends. The dogs were veterans of many Alaskan miles and the two adventurers had years of open country living. The grandmothers of Iqaluit had seen that the abominable Americans' coats needed softening, so they got together and had a party. They sat in a circle, had cookies and tea, and chewed on their coats. Made them as soft as suede shirts.

The arrival of the adventurers had a profound effect on us. Through sheer size and force of personality they cut a swath through the fragile personalities of the DEW Liners. They were doing something. We were sitting and watching equipment. This must have been how the first farmers felt, standing by their miserable crops of grain watching the hunters go out to do battle with the woolly mastodons.

We loved the action and the adventure they personified. They were going somewhere. They were off to Clyde River, then to Nanasivik. They carried the great adventure with them, like their well-chewed coats. We wanted to see an adventure. They wanted to live an adventure. We were locked in a world just as closed and insular as any submarine at the bottom of the sea. They were on the sea, riding the waves, braving the storms. They made us feel less alive. But slowly, flaws began to appear in their lives.

We asked them questions about their homes, families, wives, trying to gain some connection, some understanding, however tenuous, to the lives of career adventurers. Details were sketchy and pretty much as we expected. A couple of wives, a couple of kids they hadn't seen in a while. A sense of smugness came over some of us as we realized somebody had to pick up the tab for a lifetime of adventuring. We conveniently forgot that most of us had a couple of wives and a couple of kids we hadn't seen in a while.

It was as if some very rich and very powerful relative had visited, giving us a glimpse of another life beyond our safe and secure rut. Then, having shown us the world beyond our noses, they slammed the door in our faces and left. They had placed a mirror to our lives and shown us our boredom, our aimlessness, our lives unlived. For that we resented them.

Was the purpose of their trip purely adventure? Or was it an extreme attempt at escape from the mundane, the boring, the tedious? Were they running towards something or away from something? We never asked. If we had to ask that question we would never have understood the answer. We stood in a group. Although they travelled together, they stood separately.

The preparation for departure started almost immediately. They wanted to make a dash to Clyde River two hundred miles up the coast. There they could fish, replenish their stores, and empty bellies, and maybe acquire a couple more dogs. They were running out of time. They had to make Clyde. You could see it in their faces and hear it in their voices. Like it was the Holy Grail. That was when we realized this trip was scaring the piss out of these guys. They had four days to rest and get ready. They needed four weeks. Worried glances were exchanged between them as they spoke of the dogs, which were just about finished. The cook gave them every extra scrap of meat he could spare. Men would order two steak dinners, eat half of one, and walk over and scrape their plates out the window to the waiting huskies. Clyde River was two hundred miles north. At twenty miles a day, they could be there in ten or eleven days. If their luck held out.

A Caribou twin engine sits on the strip at the
Cape Hooper DEW site.

After four days of clean sheets, rest, and meat for the dogs, it was time to go. On the day they left it was so cold ice crystals hung in the air. They looked long and hard at the overcast sky, their dogs, each other. Clyde River! The dogs passively waited to be teamed up. One after another they were belted into their harnesses. With handshakes all around, the adventurers abruptly left.

The radar site quickly got back to normal. People nestled down into the warm blanket of routine and the brush with adventure receded into the background. We worked our government-issue projects. We filled in our government-issue forms. After 5:00 PM we snuggled up in the government-issue armchairs in the government-issue lounge and watched videos, pushing time behind us, waiting for our freedom. We marked our calendars, counted our sleeps, and rehearsed our own departures.

Ten days later there was a flurry of activity down at the beach. They came back! They were supposed to be in Clyde! Anyone off duty piled into the Bombardier and highballed it down the slope. The radio crackled and we were told an unscheduled airplane was coming from Clyde. Destination, Iqaluit. What had happened?

A whiteout had happened. They had sat in their tent for days, behind an iceberg, trying to outlast the storm. When they went outside to relieve themselves, the visibility was so bad they had to hold onto the tent with one hand or they could get lost and freeze mere feet away.

In the Antarctic, Sir Walter Scott and his men had starved to death in a whiteout six miles away from food. Our adventurers almost suffered the same fate. Whenever there were lulls in the storm, they could see the lights of our radar site twenty miles away, high up on the cliff. At night, ice crystals and howling snow would take those lights and smear them, dance with them, making them appear closer than they really were.

They lay in their freezing tent with the sides rattling in the blizzard and dreamed of home, warmth, and our safe outpost. Supplies dwindled away and two more dogs died of cold and starvation. The frost burns on their cheeks and noses were enough to make a strong man wince. When they talked, their cracked lips oozed blood. As the small one spoke to us, his face screwed up and he turned to concentrate on arranging the bundles for the return trip home to Alaska. There was a crackle in his voice. The dogs were part of his family. They had suffered and died for his daring. The team was not only smaller in number, it was smaller in size. The survivors retreated into themselves.

We stood around the bustle like spectators at a traffic accident. Flashes of raw emotion from the adventurers embarrassed us. We offered lame help and were awkward. In their hurried efforts to leave, we saw a flicker of our fate if ever the giant engines in the powerhouse died and we had to walk out of this cold and lonely place. How long would we last out on the land? With our hoods up and the fur hiding our eyes, we were glad no one could see our faces.

The plane that took them out was called a Caribou. The adventurers had looked for days for a caribou to hunt down to feed the dogs. The little two-engine fluttered out of the sky about noon. Even though it was a small jump to the open door of the plane, the dogs were so weak they had to be lifted, one by one. The sleds were loaded. With a quick, sad wave, the adventurers climbed in. The plane rattled and hummed as it passed us standing beside the strip. Picking up speed, it rose over the ice and banked, bound for home. We silently piled back into the Bombardier for the long bounce back up the trail to the site. And the routine.

Their goal was to circumnavigate Baffin Island by dog team. They only got about a third of the way around. Was it a failure? That depends. If you have the soul of an adding machine and only count the miles put behind them, sure they failed, and miserably at that. If you look at the spirit of adventure, of quest, of attempting the grand plan, then it wasn't a failure at all. It was a success of the best kind, the kind that says we won't talk about it, we won't dream about it, dammit, we'll just go out and try it.

You saw them in the arctic half-light, and then they were gone. A movement out of the corner of your eye—nothing more. But not that bear. There was something wrong with that bear. He was not like the others. He wanted in.

Cape Dyer, on Baffin Island, is a DEW station and weather radar site situated exactly six miles north of the Arctic Circle. It was one lonely outpost, holding the record for the worst weather on the DEW Line. The eighteen-hour arctic nights increased the sense of isolation.

A bear showed up one day at the tail end of a blizzard that had moaned its funeral dirge for almost a week, dumping several feet of snow onto the airstrip and approach to the hangar. To go outside was foolish, to attempt to clear the airstrip was suicide. So we sat in our warm cocoon and waited. We did a lot of that at Cape Dyer.

Other bears had come and gone all season—it was no big event for us. They wandered through silently, like half-seen sharks in a blue-black ocean. You saw them in the dim arctic light, and then they were gone. A movement out of the corner of your eye—nothing more. But not that bear. There was something wrong with that bear. He was not like the others. He wanted *in*. He kept circling the buildings, over and over again. For the next few days, the PA system was constantly on.

"Heeee's baaaaack! And he's at the kitchen."

The bear would circle in the fading light and glistening

snow, and when someone moved, he'd jog over to see if there was anything or anyone for lunch. The first day he mostly stayed around the dining hall, smelling the stairs, sniffing the doors—shopping. The huskies went crazy. They would circle him at a safe distance, barking. Once in a while one would get too close and the bear would lunge. The more agile dogs would leap back to a safer distance. It became a deadly game of tag. At first it was entertaining for us to watch—we were so bored from the blizzard. We expected him to leave, but he never did. At four o'clock the first morning, a voice screamed into the PA system.

"THERE'S A BEAR IN THE ATB! THERE'S A BEAR IN THE ATB!"

We stood shivering in our underwear, watching helplessly out the window as the bear attacked the weather office in the airport terminal building across the courtyard. Standing under the glow of the amber light, he ripped at the window with his teeth and claws, then reached in and pulled something back.

"THE DRAPES, HE'S GOT THE DRAPES! It's only the drapes."

The bear stood down and ripped at the heavy black cloth and vinyl. Hopping back up, he pulled out the drape rods, the window sash, and other parts of the surrounding wall with his teeth, then crawled into the building where the night weatherman was working. We stood stone-still.

"Holy shit . . . holy shit . . . holy shit," someone kept muttering.

I felt sick. I'd experienced many fears before but nothing like this. Long minutes passed before the bear re-emerged from the window and climbed down to the snow. Sniffing the air, he left the amber glow, disappearing as quickly as if someone had shut off the light. Minutes later the weatherman came bursting out the back door of the building. He had been saved because the back door to the weather office opened into the outer office where the bear was. The animal couldn't quite get at the weatherman, who was cowering in the storage area. From then on the bear had our undivided attention.

The only good thing about the second day was that the storm broke and the weather started clearing up. We were able to see the bear circling. The station chief broke the seal on the locker of the bear crackers, and anyone who had reason to go outside took several. Bear crackers, or thunder flashes, are a cross between a percussion grenade and a firecracker. If they explode in your hand you lose fingers. Every time the bear barged into the camp, which he did many times, he was greeted by multiple explosions. If one landed close to him, he'd run off about a block, shake his head, sit down for awhile, and then come right back. We spent that night quietly, each in his own room, listening and waiting. No bear had ever tried to break in before, but this one didn't play by the rules.

The next morning was quiet and bright. At five-thirty, Darryl the cook walked to work across the courtyard. Suddenly he and the bear saw each other. Visualize this: Darryl was on third, the bear and dogs were on first, and home plate was the safety of the kitchen door. Darryl reached light speed almost instantly. As the sprinting bear began to cut the angle on him, he was shocked to see how fast a polar bear could run. For the last twenty feet of the deadly foot race, the bear and Darryl were running almost directly at each other. Bear and cook hit the stairs at the same time. Through the railing of the stairs, the bear lunged at Darryl. After the first step, Darryl jumped over and around the snapping head. As his foot hit the fourth step, he grabbed the latch of the door and yanked—the wrong way. Six months of coming through that door and he yanked down instead of up. Recovering quickly, our cook jerked open the door, escaping just as the first paw swung around. We had scrambled eggs for breakfast.

Lunchtime found most of us in the dining hall. The sound of faraway barking meant our friend was occupied elsewhere, and that felt good. After a while, however, the barking got louder and louder. Then he appeared. He was hungry and we were to be his lunch. He sniffed at the door, the tinkling wind chimes, the steps. His solid black eyes looked up at us all standing in the windows. It was not a pleasant stare. A couple of thunder flashes and he ran away, but not far.

After that, we all had a very animated discussion about just who the endangered species was here. We all wanted to leave the bear alone, but nobody had ever seen one this aggressive.

"I didn't spend all those years studying the environment to start shooting endangered species."

"But he's trying to kill us, for pete's sake!"

"So we'll just stay inside for a few days."

"But he's coming in the bloody windows!"

"Maybe he'll just get fed up and go away."

"That's what I'm worried about!"

"Yeah, he wants to eat ME!"

The station chief told us the next plane to make it in would bring an Inuit hunter. He could handle the bear. This was cold comfort because our airstrip was under three feet of snow and so were the alternate strips.

While the crew worked constantly with the caterpillar tractors and snowplows to clear the snow, we were to protect ourselves as best we could. But the thunder flashes were having less and less effect—whenever the bear came close to the open-cab tractor, the operator would rev the motor and put the dozer blade in his face.

My project was finished and I was waiting for the plane to take me to another site.

Everybody but the cook, janitor, and station chief were out cleaning the runways. The chief grabbed me and led me to one of the offices. He unlocked a cabinet and we stared at two old USAF M1 Garands. Up until that moment I had not known there were any weapons on that site other than a flare gun. This was the first time I'd ever seen a rifle on a radar base. The chief looked at me and I looked at him.

"Do the Russians know we have these?"

"Never mind the wisecracks. Do you know how to use this?"

"It looks like my dad's old Lee-Enfield."

Although my father had owned a rifle, I never shot it. I hadn't killed an animal since I snared a gopher in Moose Jaw when I was eleven. I got the job of guarding the camp because I was the only non-essential person not clearing the airstrip. I was also too stupid to realize what was going to happen.

And so the great white hunter, armed with his USAF M1 Garand circa 1965 (the year I entered high school), set out to protect the Dye Lower DEW Line site. I really didn't think I'd have to shoot the rifle, but I made up some simple rules. Outside the perimeter of the buildings the bear was free to wander at will. Inside the compound, trying to eat people (which he so wanted to do), he was going to get shot. Maybe I'd only shoot him after he'd bitten someone. Maybe he'd only bat someone around a bit. Maybe I should wait for the hunter.

For the next day and a half the bear was never more than a quarter of a mile away from the buildings, always there, constantly circling. As he padded around just outside the cluster of buildings, I circled inside the courtyard. He seemed to know that I was guarding the camp. Every time I'd show myself, he'd move off around another building. The huskies also seemed to know that I was another element in the equation. They'd bark at his heels and then retreat behind me.

"Are you going to shoot that bear or walk it to death?"

"Not until he starts eating someone. The hunter is due tomorrow, anyway."

After dark, I sat inside the weather office at the desk where the bear had thrown his party two nights before. He kept coming back because it was one of the few windows in the camp that was low enough for him to climb in. It had been repaired but the weathermen were still more concerned about surprise visitors than with the prevailing high or low pressure systems. The bear got in once, maybe he'd try again. I leaned back in the chair, feet up, nice and warm, with the unloaded rifle lying across the desk. An hour later the telephone jolted me from my sleep. My ear was cold from leaning against the window.

"Rick, what are you doing?"

"Sitting here, waiting for the damned bear."

"Well, the damned bear is on the other side of your damned window!"

I turned and looked out, coming face to face with the biggest, blackest eyes I'd ever seen.

"JEEESUZZ CHEERIST!"

He'd gotten used to the constant thunder flashes but a primal scream from an hysterical, short, fat, bald Canadian really got him moving. Falling on his haunches, he backed away. I fell back, hitting the filing cabinets, and scrambled to load the rifle. The stupidity of my not having already done so was not lost on me. By the time I was ready the bear had moved off around the side of the building. Anxiety enveloped the compound for the rest of the night. At one point there was a great thud as the bear, chasing the dogs, crashed into my building. People slept fully dressed for the rest of the night.

The next morning was quiet until the PA system crackled my name, followed by a short bulletin.

"Bear in the compound! Bear in the compound!!"

I retrieved the rifle, sprinted through the warehouse, and slowly opened the door to the courtyard. It was a brilliant day—ice crystals danced in the cold stillness of the arctic air. The saddle leather of my mukluks crunching the snow broke the silence. The snow after the blizzard had the colours of blue, purple, and white. Today was a cosmic blue and pink opal.

The bear was broadside, one hundred steps away from me, facing the weather office. Two white-faced weathermen watched at the window. The huskies warily paced outside of lunging distance, out of reach of those massive paws. When the door opened the bear eyed me but slowly looked away, back to the dogs, then to the weathermen. Little puffs of condensation rose from his black muzzle, crystallizing in the sunlight. His coat was luminous. I knelt in the snow, forced myself to breathe quietly, and when the huskies were clear, shot the bear in the armpit.

The *swuck* of the bullet hitting the body at close range sounded like someone beating a rug. The bear exploded in blood. Knocked sideways off his feet and into the snow bank, he immediately recovered. He also knew who had hurt him. It was the most horrific thing I'd ever seen. The bear charged me, spewing blood from both sides. The huskies now had the scent and were close on him, nipping at his wounds. Shaking them off, he was instantly at a full run. I backpedalled up the stairs, frantically reloading the rifle. He was halfway across the compound. Running flat out, he seemed to leap out of his loose fur. Streams of blood splashed on the white ice. I fumbled with the shell and it fell to the steps. He stumbled and recovered, leaving behind great red streaks. He seemed to shudder as he ran, then fell again. He got up running and came at me again, and again he fell. Six hundred pounds of muscle, claws, and teeth hit the spot where I had just knelt. The bear's front paw folded up and his chest smashed into the hard-packed snow. He splayed forward, leaving a broad smear of blood on the ice. His right foreleg stretched out in an attempt to rise. He growled once, blood gurgling from his wounds, then was quiet. He died ten feet from me.

The huskies attacked him, biting his body, dancing away, and then biting again. The weathermen ran out from their office, collared the dogs, and, disgusted, tied them up. I took the rifle and put it on the chief's desk. I went back to my room and cried like a child.

"Why didn't the bear go away like all the others? Why did I volunteer for this? Why was it so easy?"

We didn't touch the bear. We picked him up with a fork-lift and dumped him unceremoniously into a crate addressed to the Conservation Officer at Broughton Island. There was a lot of interest in why he had been so aggressive. Rabies? Worms? Starvation?

The RCMP wanted to examine the bear, and they wanted a report from the person who killed it. The crate and I were to fly on the next available plane to Broughton Island for an appointment with the law.

Next day, the long-awaited airplane arrived. The Inuit hunter who was to have shot the bear inspected the crate. He was short and gnarled; a cigarette hung out of his mouth. Typical of older Inuit, he said very little.

"Did you say a prayer for the bear?"

"No, but I was quite upset."

"You'll always have to watch out now, because the bear's *innua* (soul) will look for you."

He didn't say anything more—didn't need to. He looked into my eyes. There was a long pause.

The snow snapped under my mukluks on the path to the warehouse. The crate was waiting to be loaded on the plane. Leaning against it, I said in a half whisper: "Look, ah, bear. I really hope it's not too late but I hope your spirit is at rest. Look, I'll remember you for the rest of my life. Please forgive me. Jeez, I'm sorry. I'm so sorry. God, here I am talking to a box with a dead bear in it."

I wiped my wet face. The forklift operator gunned his motor to get me to move.

I got the job of guarding the camp because I was the only non-essential person not clearning the airstrip. I was also too stupid to realize what was going to happen.

*While we had slept warm in our bunks, six-hundred pounds
of death had ghosted past, a blue-white form following
the scent laid down by a seal.*

There were no fences, telephone poles, or tufts of dead grass peeking through the drifts. In every direction, as far as every horizon, it was flat, featureless snow. I glanced to the north, where the white condensation cloud from the radar site's powerhouse wafted over the rise, breaking the unending line of sky and snow. That cloud was my lodestar, my way home. It was the one feature in an otherwise featureless plain. The longer I spent at that radar site, the more I relied on its puff of smoke on the horizon.

I waited, listening to the *potato-potato-potato* of the truck's exhaust idling away precious fuel. Angled away from the truck was a snow mound that stretched out for a mile, lined with blue lights. The International Airport. I snorted.

My mukluks crunched on the frozen surface of the airstrip. The hundred-degree drop in temperature from the truck's interior to the bald Arctic struck a physical blow. My toque started to steam. Shaking like a bird rearranging its feathers, I searched the sky. Jenny Lind Island. One hundred miles east of Cambridge Bay, one hundred miles west of Gjoa Haven. At first glance Jenny Lind was a bald, barren sand mound, stuck alone in the middle of the Arctic Ocean. After four months of living there it was still a bald, barren, sand mound in the middle of the Arctic Ocean.

I stiffened. Far to the west a black spot appeared on the horizon. Once a week that black spot brought smiles to the crew. It grew, taking the shape of an airplane. It hummed, grated, and rattled overhead as it made the wide turn into the airstrip, fluttering down using only a third of the available area. DHC 6 DEHAVILLAND TWIN OTTER (PG. 33).

"That Caribou could land in my backyard," I thought to myself.

The silver and white plane taxied to the end of the strip where I waited. I tightened my jacket against the wash from its propeller. The engines whined down, leaving a vacuum of sound until the truck's gentle idle once again filled the air. The pilot waved and opened his window.

"One passenger, buncha food, and mail. Datzit, datzol."

"Any good lookin' women on board?"

"Ya had your chance last month, there was one over at Cape Dyer. Still had most of her teeth. Maybe it's time to go home and visit mama. How long you been up on this garden spot of the Arctic?"

"Too long," I chuckled. I felt the strange sensation of a smile.

The truck was quickly backed up to the side of the plane and the carefully labelled packages transferred into its open box.

Once loaded, we didn't dawdle—our cargo would freeze quickly at forty below. The whole operation took less time than a coffee break. Pulling away, we turned to face the plane's departure. With a quick wave from the pilot, engines at full scream, the Caribou accelerated down the runway and veered off into the sky.

The new man was young, eager, and a little intense. He sniffed the musty air. After a few questions there was a pause in the conversation. I was near the end of my rotation and had become accustomed to speaking in one-word sentences. I was used to the silence. The conversation flickered in and out, creating long pauses. Both of us stared awkwardly at the track in the snow. Suddenly he brightened.

"Didja hear? They got the hostages out."

I stared at him. "What hostages?"

"The ones that's been flying all over the Mediterranean for the last two weeks."

"Never heard."

He searched my face to see if I was kidding him. My expression put that notion in doubt.

"C'mon, every TV and newspaper in the world was full of it. They played it all day long. You never heard?"

"Nope."

"Shoot, for the last two weeks I've been glued to the TV. Watching them go from place to place, airport to airport. My grass didn't get cut. I had dinner in front of the tube. My wife's screaming at me. The kids whining. I missed their hockey game to watch it on the tube. Got up a couple of times in the night to watch CNN. There were news bulletins and diagrams and on-the-spot reporting. You sure you didn't hear about it?"

"Not much TV up here. There's CBC North radio if you like the sound of static."

"Well, the whole world was watching. The terrorists took 'em all over the Mediterranean, bargaining with the CIA or somebody like that. Pretty dramatic. Gee, everybody watched. Nobody talked about anything else. There were talk shows about what the terrorists demands were, all that media stuff.

There were hundreds of media trailers at the airport. Nobody talked about anything else. I got into a big shouting match with my brother-in-law. He wanted to just shoot 'em. Idiot. I got right into it. My wife said she was glad I was leaving. You guys never heard about it? You sure?"

I shrugged my shoulders.

"All the news we get is in those bags you came with."

"No radio, no TV. Maybe I'll phone home when I get settled. Find out what happened."

"Nobody died? Everybody just chased this plane all over the place?"

"Well no, nobody died. But it was close. It coulda happened!"

The black truck bounced over a frozen rise, rumbling along the faint trail. Silence filled the cab. An arctic fox suddenly appeared, side-stepping off the road in front of us. With none of the graceful amble of a polar bear or the prance of a caribou with his head held high, it shuffled and shambled like a savvy street kid on the make. His white coat blending completely with the snow, he appeared and disappeared before our eyes. I brought the truck to a stop and we craned our necks for another glimpse. The new man busily clicked away with his camera.

"Too bad you didn't bring your camera."

"Ah, I got lots of pictures. Now I just watch. Don't have to worry about focusing or any of that shit. I just remember. You gotta watch when you leave the site for foxes. A lot of them got rabies. Always take a stick, a big friggin' stick. Once they got rabies, they go nuts. I've seen them bite the wheel of a truck. Poor bastards, running around the site just goin' nuts. You wanna shoot 'em to put 'em out of their misery."

"Pain?"

"Oh yeah, their brain rots, it's just pain. You can see it in their eyes, pain. Always take a stick."

He nodded quickly.

Further on we crossed the tracks of a polar bear that had pigeon-toed his way past the site. While we had slept warm in our bunks, six hundred pounds of death had ghosted past, a blue-white form following the scent laid down by a seal.

"Once saw a polar bear flip a three-hundred-pound seal out of a hole in the ice like a bottle cap. Musta shot him in the air six feet. Nobody dies of old age out here in the wild."

Far off, distant spots moved in a rhythm as old as time. The new man followed my gaze.

"Caribou."

"Geez, there's hundreds of them."

"Wolves must have killed something. When the wolves are hunting, the caribou bunch up. No wolves today."

The truck slowed over a frozen stream. We talked about the taste of arctic char in the spring. I pointed out where the local flock of Canada geese nested each summer and where to get the best pictures of the yellow balls of fluff that were their young. I talked about the foxes and the wolves and the other birds that preyed on them, and how their parents protected them with everything they had, even their lives.

We slowed to see if the musk-ox were still in the neighbourhood. With their long, shaggy hair, it was hard to see their legs. When they ran, they flowed over the landscape. If pursued by wolves, they would skid to a stop and form a circle around their calves, facing out to stare down the menace. The wolves that followed the herd never gave up, never let them rest. The herd was always on the watch, always scared.

At a rise overlooking the frozen bay I stopped the truck to look where the water remained open year-round, despite the blistering cold. The currents of the Arctic Ocean would speed up over a submerged reef, wearing away the ice. A steam cloud rose over the opening. Sometimes at freeze-up whales would get trapped there, easy picking for bears. For days, maybe weeks, all you'd see was black forms moving in the water, with huge pink and white chunks ripped out of them. The ice around the hole would be splattered pink. Then the water would be still.

The three-mile ride had taken the better part of an hour. We slowly whined up the last incline to the radar site. With grinding gears, the truck reached the buildings. Truck doors slammed as we got out to unload the week's now-frozen packages.

The loading dock doors rattled open. Through a cloud of condensation, the starched-white cook appeared. Motioning to where the packages of food should be placed in the vestibule, he turned to the warm kitchen.

I caught his eye and nodded in the direction of the new man.

"Got a new mouth to feed, Cookie. Treat 'im good, he's been held hostage."

I tripped and sprawled on the floe, scraping my bare hands on ice crystals. The sounds of Canada Day celebrations on the beach echoed and wavered far behind me. Looking up, I studied the hulk of the old ship. Like a beacon it stood visible from every point in the harbour. It was old, ugly, and dead, but not buried. It was a ghost. In response to my thoughts, the wind whipped a wire and played a moaning tune.

The sky was a deep cobalt blue. Bright, brittle sunlight shone sideways across the ice. The sun is never directly overhead in the Arctic. It skips around the horizon in a circle, confusing the unwary southerner. Shadows stretch out forever. Looking south towards the sun a visitor feels a pale and fragile warmth, in the shade a hint of the true arctic cold, still and deadly. The half of the ship in the bright sunlight was depressing, the other half forbidding. A silent, cold silhouette.

Years ago, the ship had run aground in a storm. Like the CN Tower in Toronto or the Lion's Gate Bridge in Vancouver, it had become a local fixture. It stood as a silent sentinel at the water's edge. If you ever walked the Hall Beach main street and looked towards the ocean, you would

The abandoned ship in the harbour of Hall Beach.
Vandalism, fire, and years of abandon had left very little.

see a row of small houses, a desolate ship, and another row of houses.

The shifting ice on that summer's day had spaces that could open and swallow a man. If you fell in it would slowly close over, pushing you down into its trap. The last conscious thing you would see was the blue-white underside of the floe, lazy and indifferent to your screams of terror.

I jumped over the leads in between the ice packs and scrambled along, keeping an eye on the rotten ice ridges. Momentarily the wind carried the sounds of the celebration, the distant roar of all-terrain vehicles racing up and down the sandy beach, mixed with the murmur and laughter of the Inuit children. The safety and security of the beach were getting further away. This was stupid. Nobody deserves to die, but some people seem to push it. I was pushing it. It had seemed like such a short distance when I started out. How many open leads of water had I jumped? Five? Six? How many patches of rotten ice had I avoided? How many chances to drown?

Finally standing on the last floe, I rested my hands against the cold steel sides of the ship. There was no movement in the hull. It was to be imprisoned in this northern sandbar forever, far away from the warm and friendly oceans of the south. It had come to this place one fateful night years ago. While the crew slept, the anchors had dragged, leaving giant furrows in the sandy bottom of the bay. Giant waves had jackhammered the ship into a sandbar, breaking its back while the storm raged.

The crack was well down by the keel. It had quickly filled with water and settled the remaining few feet into the sand of Hall Beach Bay. Several attempts to pump the water from the hold had proved futile. It sat upright in very shallow water. From a distance everything looked normal. It looked for all the world as if the ship was simply awaiting a new load to deliver to the south.

The seamen had stripped and abandoned her to the locals. The curious villagers ventured out and stripped her of any remaining valuables. Souvenirs from that ship are still in houses all over Hall Beach. When nothing remained but its shell, it became an exotic party house. The local kids would go out over the ice, party all night, and then return to the safety of the shore.

Someone had pushed the ship's forklift over the edge of the hold. It had plummeted twenty feet into the murk, no doubt creating new holes. The front half of the ship was covered with a great scar of rust where a white-hot fire had raged. It had been vandalized beyond recovery, destroyed piece by piece, then finally incinerated.

To the Inuit elders and the harbourmaster the derelict ship held a dangerous cargo—a full load of diesel fuel. The harbourmaster felt it was too dangerous and difficult to unload the tank, so he lit it up. Fires were strategically placed in the engine room, galley, living quarters, and around the fuel tank. The ship was quickly consumed. Red-orange flames licked the sky and billowed black smoke for days. The water around the ship had boiled. The red steel hull had buckled, wrinkled. For miles around the locals watched the column of black smoke rise to the sky like an ancient offering on a funeral altar. It signalled the ship's death. They let it burn and burn and burn.

Torching the ship was a smart move on the harbourmaster's part because it became unattractive very quickly. The next set of kids that decided to party on it came back covered in soot.

The lowest part of the railing was about twelve feet above the ice. I grabbed a dangling rope and did my best imitation of a marine at boot camp. Twice. With much grunting and scraping, I gained the rail. Sitting on the deck, burping the remains of several beer from the party on the beach, I looked at what was left of the ship. Vandalism, fire, and years of abandonment had left very little. Looking aft from amidships, a hole that used to be a door opened like the terrified mouth in the painting *The Scream*. Beyond was only black and decay. The cabins and crew quarters were charred skeletons. Wires and burnt insulation hung from the ceiling in the galley. Melted forks and spoons littered the floor in splashes of silver and black. A brilliant white wall, miraculously untouched by fire, stood out in sharp contrast, a testament to what once was.

A breeze came off the land, bringing with it the rattle of an ATV. The charred remains hanging from the ceiling swayed in the wind. The noise died down, leaving only the humming whisper of the wire on deck. I shivered. The sound undulated, playing with my ears. It resonated in the pit of my stomach, even though that particular pit was still full of beer.

Wary of the massive holes in the galley's floor, I walked out of the cabin to the stern. Away from the sun it was cold and still. With only the Arctic Ocean to look at, I could hear, smell, and taste the dead ship. It whispered again.

The engine room was visible through rotten holes in the galley's floor. Anything below was burnt past recognition. Aluminum parts had melted and dripped like wax candles. Steel had buckled and rusted like scar tissue. Here and there spots of white paint shone through where the fire had missed. The huge engine was half submerged in ice. Deep inside the ship, it had never melted.

The view if the abandoned ship from Hall Beach.
Like the CN Tower in Toronto or the Lion's Gate Bridge in Vancouver, it had become a local fixture.

Climbing above the pilothouse, I looked down the length of the abandoned hulk. This had been the captain's view. Everything looked derelict, tired, dead.

"Cheque please," I mumbled to myself. It was time to leave.

I quickly crossed the ice to the party on the beach. Leaving was a relief. It was only a ship. But it was once someone's home, business, protection from the storms.

A favourite pastime of idle mechanics and workers, sitting over their morning coffee in the cafeteria, was to try to figure out the best way to get rid of the ship. One school of thought was to seal the crack in its hull, dredge around the boat, and then re-float her. The crack would have to be sealed from the outside. Unfortunately, very few sane men would climb in a cave dredged under a ship and weld up a broken keel. Besides, a dredge ship was expensive to get, and for what? To rescue a pile of scrap iron? Another idea was to wait until the winter ice came, take a lot of torches, and cut her up. This sounded good, but the ship's bottom would still be there. Better a shipping hazard you can see than one that's cut level to the water line. Mostly, the mechanics and welders just liked to see machinery working. They hated to see it die such an undignified death.

Years passed. For me, the story of the ship became just another tale to frighten my children. Pilots in their airplanes coming from the east would see the hulk alone, abandoned, and waiting. It sat just a little offshore, to the north of the first runway light. Most people, after the initial curiosity, treated it like a derelict building on the edge of town. They ignored it. But it always had the look of a ship in the process of weighing anchor, as if it could pull up at any moment and sail south, back home to Newfoundland or Nova Scotia or Boston. It seemed to be waiting.

One foggy, wet morning, Hall Beach awoke to find the ship gone. It was as if the residents of New York City woke up to find that the Statue of Liberty had disappeared during the night. Not toppled over, not dismantled, but disappeared, gone. People came from the village, the DEW site, and the airport. They stood by the water and stared. Picture-perfect stewardesses with their eight-hundred-dollar parkas stood beside humble Inuit trappers. The whole village gathered by the water's edge. They stared out across the silent Arctic Ocean.

The whites stood in groups laughing nervously, gesturing towards the water, offering perfectly rational explanations of what had happened. The Inuit, more in tune with the moods and the feelings of the land, stood silent.

The military sent out a search plane. Well out in Foxe Basin, although it was covered in a dense fog, the crew detected a hard object on the plane's radar. The blip was heading south, out to sea. And then it vanished.

It is entirely plausible that the ice pack could have come in with the evening's tide and scooped the ship and its anchors off the bottom. Ice, frozen in the hole in the ship's bottom, could have formed a plug, keeping the seawater out and the ship afloat. A stiff offshore wind could have pushed her, still stuck in the ice pack, out to deeper water. Then the currents of Foxe Basin would have sent the ship out towards the open waters of the south. Eventually, wave action would have broken up the floe she was carried on. The ice plug that sealed the hole would have popped out and the ship would have sunk.

In the darkness of that arctic night, if the wires that I had heard humming were still attached, they would have played their low hum, like a distant lonely foghorn, as a final farewell to the land.

While the village slept, in the black fog and moaning wind, the ship silently faded into the night. If no human hand would steer her home, she would do it herself.

A long black line snaked over feature-less white. In some places, the howling arctic wind had hard-polished the snow so that it easily held a man. Here, the only sound came from the dozens of hob-nailed boots squeaking and shuddering on the icy crust. Occasionally, the stiff, frozen boots broke through, dragging the men down, momentarily halting the march. In some places the line was bunched where men carried supplies, lifeboats, and each other. In other places, long gaps appeared. There, men too weak to carry much more than themselves shambled on, one stooped figure after another. The best that England had produced, now stripped to a stuttering black line in the snow. When their exhausted bodies could no longer endure the brutal cold, the suffering, and the dread, they fell into the snow and died.

They had left the warmth of their homes and sweethearts and set out on a grand adventure. The two ships of the expedition weighed anchor to the sounds of bands and speeches. The stout ships, made from the best oak in England, were to bully their way through the ice packs of the fabled Northwest Passage. Once through, they would sail down the long coast and round the tip of South America. It was history they were making. It was fame and glory they were seeking.

Unfortunately, it was disease and death they got. The very earth and water fought them. The first winter the ice was impassable. They couldn't go forward, and worse, they couldn't go back. So they stayed in that icy hell, huddled in their ships. The killer cold enveloped them, grinding their spirits down. By the second winter the pall of starvation hung over them. Finally, icebergs the size of castles crushed their ships into kindling, forcing them to leave. They formed a line and slowly started to walk south. To the east, across a smooth, white plain, the land gently rose to a low hill. On top of that low hill, looking down on the sad procession, stood small black figures dressed entirely in animal fur.

Jenny Lind Island is a fat, pork chop-shaped island directly north of the Saskatchewan/Manitoba border. It is home to a DEW Line site. White dome, grey slate-covered buildings, blue-black trucks. In the brief moment laughingly referred to as summer, the melting snow reveals its grey rocks and green mosses surrounded by the stark blue-grey of the ocean. Just out of sight from Jenny Lind, across the sullen arctic water, lies another island that holds the bones of the Franklin Expedition.

The site at Jenny Lind is a good walk from the gravel beach. Far enough for a bored worker, fishing rod in hand, to pass a Sunday afternoon. As I neared the beach a small, round figure came into view, hovering over an aluminium boat. We exchanged waves and I walked over to the man. It was George, the Inuit who lived with his family by the radar site.

What you saw was what you got with George. Not much for small talk but always generous with his knowledge of the

Franklin's ships will never be found in any recognizable form. Crushed by
ice, their remains would have spread all the way down M'Clintock
Channel, from Cape Felix on past King William Island.

land. He wore a battered baseball cap, a gift from an American air force sergeant he had taken fishing. A shoe-leather face, red and black plaid jacket, worn black pants, and black rubber boots were George's constant summer uniform. He didn't have an opinion about politics, fashion, or international affairs. But he could show you where the fish were, how to skin a seal, and how to build a shelter to get out of the weather from literally nothing.

"Going fishing, George?"

"No. Ice comin' in."

I looked out into the bay and beyond. All I could see were the waters of the quiet Arctic Ocean. He must have been joking. The closest ice was in the bar at the radar site. Not a ripple of wind, not a cat's paw ruffled the water. If there was ice it had to be a hundred miles away. He must have been pulling my pink white leg.

"I'll bite. How can you tell there's ice coming in?" I said, a little too flippantly.

If George took offence, he never showed it. He stood still and looked up into the low mist and grey cloud that was a constant summer feature of the Arctic. His old brown finger directed my gaze toward the sky.

"See d' clouds? Where der's white, der's ice underneat."

His hand stroked the sky like a painter outlining the edges of a canvas. Following his hand I saw the gradual but distinct change between the dark-grey clouds close to us and almost pure-white clouds towards the horizon.

"Hey, that's right, you can really tell the difference. How do you know the ice is coming this way, though?"

"It wasn't der dis morning."

"Oh," I shrugged. Ask a stupid question . . .

Did Franklin and his crew know that? Did they not know how to avoid the crushing ice? Did Franklin's ships, the *Erebus* and the *Terror*, get caught in the southbound ice highway and get crushed because he and his crew didn't know this basic fact of survival in the Arctic—how to find open water? Even if they knew, they didn't stand a chance. The ice flow coming down M'Clintock Channel is relentless. Once caught, they were in the middle of a hundred-mile-wide conveyor with only one exit. In front of Cape Felix the ice impales itself on the knifepoint of King William Island. Miles of ice pile up in ridges fifty, sixty, even seventy feet high. To avoid certain death they should have crossed that meat grinder at a right angle, either as far to the east or west as possible. They didn't, and they died.

"You walkin'?" George asked.

"Yeah, I'm tired of being cooped up in the site. I've sat on my ass for three weeks. I need some exercise."

"Going far?"

Alarm bells went off.

"Why?"

"Nanuuk."

"Ah shit, polar bear? I wanted to lose weight, but not by pieces."

I looked around the surrounding dunes for cream-coloured death. My armpits began to tingle. I had lived long enough in the Arctic to not think of polar bears as cute. The sight of a three-hundred-pound seal scooped out of his breathing hole by six-inch claws, like some cap popped off a beer bottle, flashed in my memory. The radar site suddenly seemed a long way off.

"Where is it?"

George motioned towards the shore off to the right. Just where I had planned to do some beachcombing.

Franklin's ships will never be found in any recognizable form. Crushed by ice, their remains would have spread all the way down M'Clintock Channel, from Cape Felix on past King William Island. Maybe some even floated into a quiet bay on Jenny Lind Island. I wouldn't have even known what to look for. But a polar bear would know what to look for. Me.

"Well, then, I'm gonna go back. You coming?"

"No, I'm gonna finish up here."

"You want me to stay?"

George needed a city boy like me around like General George Custer needed another Sioux warrior. He shook his head. I turned to go. I hoped the government-issue parka hid most of the yellow stripe down my back. George wanted to say something, but I wanted to be safe inside the compound of the radar site, the sooner the better.

"Watch d' Caribou."

I gave him a blank stare.

"If you see Caribou all d' way around you, you're OK. Der's no bear. If you see a place where der's no Caribou, dat's where d' bear is."

A simple warning from an Inuit might just have saved my life. Did the Franklin Expedition seek out the advice of the locals? Were the two ships a cocoon that gave the sailors a false sense of protection? I thought of the steak and lobster meal we would be having that Sunday at the site. If we ever had to walk out of here, the menu would change. We would only eat what we could carry. How many tins of contaminated bully beef could a sailor from the Franklin party, weakened by months of starvation, carry? Far in the distance the white, gleaming radar dome of the DEW site stood out against the grey sky. Safety was there. TV, cookies, coffee, bedrooms, lazy conversations, laughter. I'll bet the sailors of the Franklin Expedition thought of their ships the same way. They had brought their civilization with them. When they lost the ships they lost that civilization. They then had to deal with the reality of the Arctic. It's littered with the bones of white men who set out to conquer it.

You do not conquer the Arctic—you survive it. You float on its surface like a piece of foam on a sea wave. Stand with your hands on your hips daring the Arctic to do its worst and it does. Your last miserable days are spent grovelling in the snow eating your shipmate's leg, just to make it through another day. It wasn't until a Norwegian named Amundsen lived with the natives and ate what they ate and saw what they saw that Europeans started to endure the Arctic.

I stood hesitantly in front of George, one part of me wanting to run away, back to the safety of the buildings, to my white cocoon. Another part of me, the curious tourist, wanted to stay with the old Inuit. To cover my fear I asked a question that I thought would get a simple no, so that I could just say goodbye and leave, taking with me some semblance of dignity.

"Say, George, do your people ever talk about the Franklin Expedition? You know, the guys that died around here last century?"

George looked at my face, my feet, then away.

"Sometimes. Lot of people looked for dem."

"Did the Inuit help them? Some people say a couple of the sailors lived for a while with the local clan."

"Dey tried to help, d' whites chased dem away. Crazy."

"Is that true? How do you know? Did that really happen? What happened?"

George looked away, startled by my outburst. I peppered him with more questions. Bear forgotten, I advanced, trying to gain any nugget of information, anything. George retreated into centuries of silence.

"George, don't let me hang here . . . what happened?"

He looked away. His part of the conversation was over.

George busied himself with the boat. After an embarrassing period of silence, I changed the subject. He looked relieved. I had just gotten a flash of Inuit history, a tiny flicker. I wanted more. I wanted as much information as I could get. I wanted as much of the story as George could give in a lifetime. I wanted everything, and no commercials.

It just wasn't going to happen. Getting George to pull up a chair, light a pipe, and entertain me with a long oration of the Inuit version of the last days of Sir John and the boys simply was not to be. It would have been easier getting a fish to tap-dance. I surrendered to the inevitable.

Centuries of survival have hammered into the Inuit the need to live for now—only worry about today. Don't waste anything—don't clutter up your life with things that hinder basic survival. Don't even think about things that get in the way of the next meal. The danger of the bear is today, the food that the caribou provides is today, the fish, the birds, the way the ice moves are all today. Survival is all that matters. Survival is today. Sir John Franklin and his men are, well . . . history. Their deaths were unfortunate, but not that significant in the eyes of a people who live with simple survival as a daily constant.

I left him at the aluminium whaleboat. George never again talked about the Franklin Expedition, and I never asked. I walked back over the road with a worried eye on the caribou. Half-way to the radar site I stopped and looked back to the bay. George was standing by the battered silver boat, looking out to sea. I followed his gaze out to the horizon. An hour ago the water had been black and sombre. Now it was ghostly white. Broken in spots, bunched up in others, but definitely a long line of white. A cold, biting wind had picked up. The ice was moving in.

Arctic Ocean

Chukchi Sea

Beaufort Sea

Dead Horse City
Prudhoe Bay
Kaktovik

McKinley Bay

Tuktoyaktuk

ALASKA

YUKON

Arctic Circle

NORTHWEST
TERRITORIES

NUNAVUT

Hudson Bay

Churchill

BRITISH
COLUMBIA

ALBERTA

SASKATCHEWAN

MANITOBA

ONTARIO

0   250 km

PART TWO
DRILL SHIP

The oil companies would abandon their drill ships to the ice at the end of the season. Come spring they would chopper teams out to start them up once again.

The arctic sun burned his eyes. Standing on the ice, the labourer squinted up at the ship. It stood still, almost sinister—a seven-hundred-foot-long lump of dead red steel frozen in six feet of white ice. No movement, no swaying on the waves, no pull at the anchors. Cheaper to leave it frozen in an arctic bay than to ship it south, it had sat dead and alone for nine winter months.

The workers walked up to where a wire-rope ladder hung down off the wall of red. The wind had scraped the side of the ship in the pattern of the ladder's rungs. The men climbed up the side, reaching the deck high above the still ice. The late winter sunlight cast long blue shadows. They waved and the helicopter that was their only escape lifted off the ice and headed back to Tuk Base.

Climbing to the wide, flat deck on the front of the ship, they collected shovels that had been placed there months ago for just this event. One after another two of the workers thudded up the stairs to a grey steel deck and started to shovel. The scrape of metal broke the overwhelming silence. The past year had been good—there was only a small drift of crunchy white snow that needed to be cleared off that wide square of steel.

Shovel after shovel was thrown over the edge of the deck to the ice seventy feet below. They threw the snow downwind. Throwing in any other direction would whip the white powder back into their faces, swirling around their heads, only to land again on the deck. After a half hour of solid work they stood up, nodding to one another. A radio was produced and a message sent.

"C'mon in."

A little while later the helicopter landed on the deck. It had been shovelled but not swept. Lumps of snow that remained whipped up and formed a fog. The shovellers stood underneath the steel helideck, resting on their wide shovels, oblivious to the mini-blizzard above them. Despite the cold, they were sweating.

Looking out to the horizon, they could see McKinley Bay, which washed up on the west coast of a thumb of land that jutted out into the water. The closest supply base was Tuktoyaktuk. Tuk Base lay southwest—about an hour as the helicopter flies. Looking east there were several capes, all jutting like crooked teeth into the ice floes. Across the first cape, a low spit of land, lay the frozen Arctic Ocean. They were alone. As alone as only a stranded ship can be.

The helicopter emptied its first passengers and hopped away from the ship, thudding its way back to Tuk for more men. The four workers would be the first of a constant shuttle of men until freeze-up, months away.

Snowdrifts covered the aisles and the paths that many feet would pound hours later. Nobody had been on these decks in months. They walked over a tabloid magazine caught in the ice. Its headlines screamed year-old scandals. Frozen in time, frozen in fact.

Lights and frozen tools in hand, they unlocked the cabin door and entered the dead, dark ship, standing for a moment in the silence. They went from a sun so bright it could damage retinas to the tarry blackness of the ship's gut. Eyes blinked and slowly adjusted. Great billows of condensation hung in the air. Their minds, normally relaxed by the familiar surroundings, were weary of the very still and deadly cold. Their boots passed the purser's open office door. Inside, a frozen plastic rose in a coffee cup bloomed in the black.

Holding their flashlights in their mittened hands, the bundled men walked a caterpillar line down the steep ladder into the frozen dark. They didn't think it was possible but it was even colder down below. Pictures of the ship in warmer climes and friendlier oceans lined the walls. Reaching the engine room, they set to work on the one motor that had been pre-chosen months ago. The steel compartment was dark and foreboding.

There were seven engines on that ship. Seven monstrous, sixteen-cylinder engines with pistons the size of garbage cans. Name-tags hung at the end of each motor gave a comforting, human presence to the bleak room: Sleepy, Dopey, Doc, Grumpy, Sneezy, Bashful, and Happy.

The men huddled around one of the massive steel walls that would soon be changed from frozen to firing. The contents of the bags they brought were laid out: batteries, oil, starter fluid, wrenches, and hope. Connecting the fresh batteries, they added warm oil and squirted alcohol into the intake. They looked at each other. The leader looked down at the upturned faces and at the massive ship's motor with bored professionalism.

"C'mon."

Twenty minutes. Twenty minutes from landing on the ship to engine-start. Icy cylinders that had just received a blast of alcohol and diesel jumped. For the first time in half a frozen year the motor barked. The exploding fuel kicked the giant cylinders and shaft over in the engine's guts. The fire in its belly took hold as the giant motor coughed, then started on its own. The sound slowly changed from a high protest to the old familiar thump of a diesel motor comfortable with its purpose. One of the mechanics patted the motor affectionately. He looked around self-consciously.

An electrical breaker switch was thrown and emergency lights all over the ship came on. The workers dowsed their flashlights and looked around the now brilliant engine room, like tourists coming home after a long trip. The condensation from their breath hung in the air, blurring the light.

Slowly, methodically, the ship came back to life. With the opening of a valve, the glycol that coursed through the firing engine's metal veins was added to the engine beside it. When it was warm, its giant pistons kicked to life. Heat began to be generated by the two giant motors, burning off the frost covering their outsides. The workers' hoods were laid back on their shoulders.

Outside on the deck, the two shovellers looked up at the ship's stack when they heard the second engine kick to life. White smoke puffed out. They exchanged glances.

"Lot's of condensation in that one."

The other man nodded.

When the engine settled down and the stack blew good black billows they smiled and talked of warm things.

With an opening of another valve, hot glycol flowed like blood through the long copper tubes that looped in a vast circuit from one end of the ship to the other. All along its path, tubes, and the radiators connected to them, clicked and ticked their personal contortions as they expanded with the hot fluid. Glycol that had made the full circuit came back to the hot engines as cold as the ice that surrounded the ship. As the hours passed the fluid heated the pipes, then the radiators, then the compartments, then the ship.

The workers in the engine room removed their outer layer. They were clad in light jackets and heavy sweaters. Checking their handheld radios and holding crumpled blueprints of the electrical system, they dispersed throughout the ship. Their radios barked staccato messages once they had reached their appointed stations. The leader grabbed a huge ceramic paddle on a bank of electrical panels. With both hands, he threw the giant switch. All over the ship lights turned on, heaters erupted, and safety lights blinked. In one room, a small radio that had been silent for six months wailed a mournful country and western tune. Outside, the ship's red, green, and white running lights flashed to life and the emergency lights turned themselves off.

Several radios crackled to attention. If there was any water from melting snow that could short out the electric system, the wary mechanics would pick it up quickly. They wandered the hallways and rooms, checking for electrical fires using the world's oldest safety devices—their eyes and noses.

In the galley, a rumble was heard. The *plunk-plunk* of the pipes pushing out gasps of air sounded. The workers watched the water in the sink trickle, cough, and slowly fill out to a steady stream. The water-maker deep inside the engine room had started its process. Like all the other equipment it would run steadily and not be shut off for the next six months. They let the water run to clear the pipes of any glycol residue.

The shovellers came in from the cold and removed their parkas, loudly blowing their noses. They joined the mechanics in the ship's galley. While the heaters had warmed the air in the room, the tables, counters, and seats were still cold. A tin of coffee was found and water from jugs carried in that morning was poured into the pot. Soon the smell of brewing coffee wafted through the galley. The crew drank it black—milk and cream would come later.

"We ready for 'em?" the leader asked, rising to his feet.

Several nods were shared. He turned and took the stairs up to the radio room. Nestled into the operator's chair, he spoke into the microphone.

"She's warm and wet and all ready for you."

Across a hundred miles of frozen tundra and ocean, a fleet of helicopters awaiting those words took off from the airstrip at Tuktoyaktuk and made its way north. It carried the sailors to man the ship, the cooks to feed the men, the labourers, the mechanics, the welders, the food, the laundry, the toilet paper, the newspapers, the spare parts. An airborne armada en route to fill a city frozen in the arctic ice. The ship had come to life.

The Americans came onboard, grabbing their duffel bags and ducking under the spinning blades of the helicopter. Tumbling off the ship's helideck, they headed down the steep ladder to the main deck. Funny how they looked like us, but we'd been onboard for a month so they smelled better. We greeted them the way groups of men have always done.

"Hey, 'Mercan, what kinda country don't let the Minnesota Vikings win the Superbowl? You gotta law somewhere that says that?"

"Hey, Kaynuk, how do you spell Canada? C–eh! N–eh! D–eh!"

"I always like that joke, every friggin' time I hears it!"

Instant friendships were made. An outsider couldn't tell who was American and who was Canadian. Except, of course, the Americans smelled better.

We Canadians were the crew on the drill ship *Explorer II*. In 1985 our vessel and a small support fleet of ice-strengthened ships were leased by an American oil company to drill in American waters off the north coast of Alaska, in Prudhoe Bay. The Canadians ran the ship, from the captain through the

When we were anchored we were a Canadian ship. When we were drilling we were an American port. The governments said that the drill pipe was a permanent structure and the moment it touched the seabed it changed us from a Canadian ship to an American port.

mates and ordinary sailors down to the lowest level, the ship's welder. I was the ship's welder.

The Americans were the drill crew. From the ramrod down to the lowest labourer, they operated the drill rig and the equipment. The plan was that the Canadians would get the fleet there. Once on site, the Americans were to look for oil. Our governments had other plans.

"Doc, I gotta toof ache."

"You American or eh-team?"

"'Mercan."

"Then you gotta go wake up the American doc. I'm Canadian."

"Whatzzit matter what I am? My toof aches."

"'Americans are not allowed to have codeine without a prescription, Canadians are. Codeine's all I got. Go wake up the American doc."

"You mean we got two docs on board?"

"Yeah, one for the Americans and one for the Canadians."

"But my toof don't care, it hurts now."

Slowly, the two crews started to find out that cooperation, respect, and friendship were one thing, government regulations were another. Both had the gung-ho attitude of "Let's get the job done." The government's attitude was "Let's not."

"Chief, I gotta offload some of these crates to one of the supply boats so's I can weld the crack in the deck. Could you radio one of them to swing by?"

"Sorry, can't do it until we stop drilling."

"Why, it's only a couple of crates—it'll only take a couple of minutes."

"It's not the time, kiddo, it's the regs. Ya see, when we're anchored we're a Canadian ship. When we're drilling we're an American port. The governments say that the drill pipe is a permanent structure and the moment it touches the seabed it changes us from a Canadian ship to an American port. No to the crates. If a ship lands while we're drilling, he has to pay port entry fees, customs duties, and all kinds of crud. It's just not worth it. Wait an hour or two."

"Aw, come on, who's to know?"

"Those two," motioning with his chin to two figures by the railing.

"You mean short and curly? Who are they?"

"Customs."

"We got two customs officers on this ship?"

"One American, one Canadian. Both assholes."

"When we're American does that mean that we have green cards?"

"Ya, the Yanks have Canadian work visas and the Canadians all get US green cards. Don't get excited though, it's only good on this ship and it expires the moment you leave."

"Well, call me when we're Canadians again, I'll be down below helping the mate. He'll be happy to know he's an alien."

Government regulations, customs regulations, environmental protection procedures, forms in duplicate, triplicate, one on top of another, again and again, started to wear the entire crew down. Grumbling started against everyone and everything that was seen to be government-related.

One bright, cold day the surreal fog of interlacing and overpowering government regulations became crystal-clear. It came in the form of an eager, pink-cheeked university graduate who was so serious and so clean he would probably never smell bad. He was a government environmental control officer, and we were the big bad oil company. Unfortunately, he was also a pretty decent sort, right up until his crucifixion.

"Hey, what are you doing?"

"What does it look like? I'm oiling the threads on the drill pipes so's they don't rust."

"Yeah, but you're slopping all that oil on the deck and it'll go over the side into the water. That's gotta change."

"Ah come on, it's only a couple of quarts spilt at most."

"Naw naw, that's gotta change."

Several days later, at unbelievable expense, a forty-five-gallon drum of environmentally friendly fish oil was delivered via chartered plane and helicopter to our awaiting crew. Now we could slop the oil over the pipe threads, ourselves, or anything else because it was all-natural. And slop we did. The smell of fish permeated the ship.

Within an hour of opening the drum, way off in the distance we saw the creamy-white head of our first polar bear bobbing in the ocean. Then came another, and another, all sniffing the air like sharks on a blood trail. The stink of rancid fish oil lured them in for what they hoped was a feeding frenzy. Men who had lived in the Arctic for years had never seen so many polar bears together at one time. Within an hour all work stopped as camera after camera came out. Men went down to the cabins to get the off-duty crew to come up and see the sight. All the support vessels stopped dead in the water to avoid hitting the bears, which swam around circling, sniffing, eager to climb aboard. At one time we counted eight bears on the port side alone.

The captain and the drill chief turned a pinky purple. The radio crackled and the very next helicopter took off with a forty-five-gallon drum of fish oil and an environmental officer.

Isaac Newton said that for every action there is an opposite reaction. The fish oil incident had a profound effect on the crew and its attitude to the stifling regulations. We became less 'Mercans or Kaynuks or drill crew or ship's crew. We became "us"—family. The government officials saw some of the regulations for what they were. Even though the rules were never dropped or circumvented, they were enforced with more common sense.

Funny thing, after all that we were the first offshore rig in Prudhoe Bay to ever discover oil.

"Hey doc, I gotta toof ache."

"You 'Mercan or Kaynuck?"

"What do you want me to be?"

The CANMAR 1 sits in dry dock. I was in the belly
of this ship when the fire broke out.

Waavoooooff! The blue and orange blast hit me in the chest and face. Throwing away the welder's cutting torch, I instinctively batted at the flames shooting past my gloves, up my sleeves, and licking my cheek. It was as useless as pushing away a wave at the beach. The fire followed my arms and wrapped around my neck. We were in dry dock and this tank was supposed to be empty!

My leather gloves started to shrivel in the fourteen-hundred-degree heat. Don't breathe! Don't suck in the flames! Get away! Get out! You're burning! You're burning up! My welding helmet started to melt. I pushed it off. The flames surrounded me. I was going to die! I was going to die inside this awful ship thousands of miles from home. Flames were even going underneath me and up my back. The blast hit me in the stomach. Hairs on my neck crackled and sputtered. My ears burned and stung. My bright-orange coveralls melted in patterns along the fold lines, igniting and turning black in an instant. I tucked my chin into my collarbone and leaned my head towards the fire as if it were a heavy rain. I had to save myself. The cloth welder's cap I wore under the missing helmet ignited. I tripped backwards and sprawled on the bottom of the tank, the flames raking over my prone body. Rising, I stumbled for the manhole. It was a seven-foot drop. I jumped to the deck of the dry dock below, landing with a thud, surrounded by the flaming diesel that washed across the floor. I fell into a crowd of men working on scaffolding under the curve of the bottom of the ship. Startled welders all yelled at the same time. They saw a huge ball of flame drop from the guts of the ship with someone flopping inside.

"Roll! Roll!" someone screamed.

Stunned workers were galvanized into action. Shouting, they gang-tackled me and started to beat out the flames, their eyes filled with panic and disbelief. Here and there, other workers froze in shock. Hands ripped at my coveralls. My face stung. I knew I was burned there. How bad, I didn't know. The lead hand charged over. He stuck his face in mine.

"What the f--- did you do? Who told you to cut those pipes?"

"You did, you dumb f--- !"

Several sets of hands reached out to stop me as I raced towards the real cause of the fire. The lead hand, unprepared for a near-death experience, suddenly backed off. A full dozen voices chimed in.

"Yeah, yeah, we heard you."

"You didn't check, did you?"

"You should have checked yourself!"

"That's your job! You told me it was empty you f---ing idiot!"

The crew obviously enjoyed the spectacle of an arrogant boss being confronted with one of his numerous mistakes in the form of a wild-eyed, still-smouldering me. With my burnt hair and blackened face, and what was left of my coveralls hanging in tatters, I resembled a very angry candlewick. I knew then that, as in war, if your leader is a fool, you usually die. At that moment I would have gladly driven my welder's pick six inches into his eye. Then I'd laugh and piss all over his grave.

It suddenly dawned on this guy that he was surrounded by several men who didn't want him on their Christmas list. Spluttering, he backed away, his eyes quickly looking at all the workers. This was a major screw up, and there were witnesses.

One of the welders with medical experience took me aside. I had been saved by the wearing of coveralls over leather, blue jeans, and long underwear. I had lost a couple of layers of skin on my ears and nose, which stung but would only require ointment. I was lucky—very, very lucky.

The lead hand marched around, eyeing the crew and me like he wanted a rematch. I was willing to go for it. This guy was dangerous.

"She's still burning!" a shout came from the hole in the side of the ship, ending the standoff.

"Jeez, that's the ship's fuel tank. If it goes, everything goes!"

Several welders gathered at the hole and peered into the gloom and smoke of the tank interior. There was a faint flickering deep in its empty cavern. The lead hand elbowed his way to the front. Trying to regain his tattered esteem, he blustered and bustled about, barking out orders.

"Get some fire extinguishers! Quick! Do I have to do everything myself?"

A red container was handed up. The welder at the hole emptied it into the gloom. White smoke covered everything and everyone. There was a tense moment while they all gathered around the open steel pit. The white mist slowly dissipated.

"It's still on fire!" the lead hand barked. "Get some more extinguishers. Quick!"

A labourer ran up with two more. The lead hand forced one from his hand. Elbowing the worker at the manhole out of the way, he shot the white cloud of the second canister into the tank. This fire was now his fire. He was going to show the crew he was still the boss. That extinguisher was emptied. The crowd of workers waited. No one spoke. Still, there was a flickering deep in the ship. One of the older hands quietly broke the silence.

"Hey, let's take a look at that fire."

"Shaddap, get me another extinguisher!" he shouted. He was regaining his tattered authority and he pressed his advantage.

By now the crew was bringing extinguisher after extinguisher. Every red-and-black canister they could find littered the deck under the ship's keel. Everything was covered in white soda. Everyone choked on the vinegary fumes. Eyes smarted and teared up. Finally, two sweating labourers rolled a three-hundred-pound extinguisher over from the front of the ship. Its steel wheels thundered on the dry dock's metal deck plates.

"Hand me the hose, I'm going in," the lead hand barked to the waiting crew.

He spoke those words like he was going "over the top in the big one." Several of the welders looked at each other. Climbing into a confined space where a fire blazed was about as wise as sticking your hand under a rock in the desert. I kinda hoped he'd do it.

"No you're not," came an order from directly behind us.

All heads turned to watch two figures walking purposefully

towards us. The commanding and rather large figure of the general foreman and a fully equipped fireman, complete with oxygen tanks and radio, approached. The crowd parted and quieted. The fireman quickly climbed up the scaffolding and disappeared into the hole in the side of the ship.

Standing amid the numerous scattered empty canisters and white mounds of soda, the general foreman surveyed the scene. The lead hand gestured in my direction. A couple of workers edged away from me. The lead hand was one thing, the general foreman was quite another.

Suddenly, the fireman's legs appeared at the manhole. The same hole that I and several gallons of flaming diesel had escaped from a half hour before. The white-powdered faces of the crew gathered around expectantly. The smiling fireman opened his gloved hand. He handed a lit flashlight to the lead hand, who stared down at it with a stunned look. It had been hanging on a wire, and its light had flickered and swung as the dry dock gently rocked in the tide. Our fearless leader had spent thirty minutes and emptied extinguisher after extinguisher trying to put out a flashlight.

The general foreman looked at the white faces of the crew, the wreckage of all the empty extinguishers, and started to slowly chuckle. It was a low, slow laugh, one that built and continued as he walked down the deck. We heard the laughter ricocheting all the way from the other end of the ship.

The guy I replaced was working from a life boat like this—
seventy feet above the Arctic ocean.

The welder hung over the side of the ship. Cables and safety line looped around him in a lazy fashion. Seventy feet below was the grey Arctic Ocean. His legs straddling the long davit for the lifeboat, he worked quickly. This was no place to spend any time. The job needed to be done, and it needed to be done fast. Coffee and buns in a warm galley would be waiting. It was hustle time. The ramrod had twice asked about this job. He'd better hurry up. Flipping his welding helmet up, he glanced out to the sea. Moored, half-hidden in the strands of arctic mist, was the rest of the fleet. He shifted position. Laying on top of the lifeboat gantry, he reached over the side to weld the last little "pickup." He hung out as far out as he dared. The welding rod melted. He stretched out more—just a little further and he'd have it. His left foot touched on a piece of steel. Using that as support, he leaned even further out, his right leg looped over the gantry.

Clack. His left foot shot downward as the piece of steel, a lever, released. The rumbling of the lifeboat and the shaking of the davit he lay on surprised him. With a thump, he felt his right leg being pressed down by something metal. His welder's helmet fell to the water below. His fingers desperately scraped along the steel as his body was dragged down the wet gantry. His eyes widened. Frantically, he pushed away from the gantry. Like the sound of a handful of dry spaghetti snapping, the gantry crackled over his leg, which shot into the air on the other side. A tangle of cable, rope, clothes, and flesh dangled over the ocean, pinned under the davits. On the other side of the gantry the welder's leg and foot stood straight up.

Across a mile of icy water, on a moored supply ship, the third mate was going for coffee and buns. He stopped and cocked his head. Above the sounds of the ship and wind he heard something. Another crew member approached him. He held his hand up to stop the mate.

"Quiet. Do you hear that?"

"What is it?"

"Hey, you guys c'mere!" He motioned for several of the crew that were passing.

"What the f--- is that?"

"Christ. Someone's screaming."

        ⋈   ⋈

It was easy to pick out my crew at the airport. We all looked about thirty-five and were styled in faded-blue-jean scruffy. There were no kiddies and no grey hairs in this crew. There were no kids because until their mid-twenties young men were still learning the trade. There was a lot more to learn than just the mechanics. If a kid showed up on a job north of the Arctic Circle he was someone's brat. Not a pleasant situation if the rest of the crew worked long and hard to earn a place. Older than fifty, they couldn't put in the hours. If they had to work the trade after fifty, chances were they had screwed up: a marriage, a business, drugs, or booze. Usually it was a combination.

A lumbering man from the construction office motioned us together in the cavernous lobby of the airport. His hair was grey. What was left of it was styled in what might have been called a pompadour. He looked out of place without coveralls and a helmet. His words were rough and to the point.

"You're going from here to Edmonton to Prudhoe Bay. There you'll split up and go to the drill ships. They're off-shore about twenty to thirty miles. You'll be going through US customs. If you got any shit on you, get rid of it now. If you get caught with drugs you will be sent back and we will charge you for the flight. And you'll never ever work for this company again."

The threat wasn't smoke. We knew a couple of welders who had been caught. They never worked the big money again. Nobody ever could prove that companies all got together to blackball the culprit, it just happened. Nothing formal was ever spoken, no letters were ever written. Someone's career evaporated with a couple of phone calls. The welders knew that the companies didn't give a lick whether they smoked enough to blow their brains out. Just don't you ever cost them money.

"Will there be fries with that order?" one of the older tradesmen chimed in. The small crowd smirked because that was code for "Your days as a $100,000-a-year welder in the Arctic are over."

The supervisor told us our assignments and the ship we were to be posted to. Motioning to me, he said:

"You'll be replacing Tom. They sent him home."

"What did he do?"

"Hurt his leg."

One of the other welders spoke up.

"He went home because he had a sore leg? That's not like him, going home for just a charley horse."

The supervisor paused for a moment.

"Naw, he pinched it. He'll probably be off for a while."

He shrugged off the rest of our inquiries and seemed glad when our flight was announced.

Alaska. Dead Horse City was the town. Prudhoe Bay was the water. Nobody ever explained why everybody who was not from Alaska called it Prudhoe Bay and not Dead Horse City. It probably just sounded better. What would you call yourself, a Deadhorsian? It got worse. Right smack in the middle of Dead Horse was a lovely little lake called Dead Chicken Lake. Apparently this place was pretty hard on farm animals.

There were stray caribou on the runway so the 737 had to circle until the airport workers shooed them out of the path with their jeep.

You couldn't go to Prudhoe Bay unless you had a place to stay. No use checking the hotels. There was one. It was booked. Always. We weren't staying around, so no reservations were needed. We got a soup and a sandwich in the hotel's restaurant. Its decor was early truck stop. It was in between flights and meals so the lunchroom was empty, except for us transients. The waitress was perky in a cautious way. She'd seen her share of horny rig pigs and their grasping hands. She had made fifty thousand dollars in tips the year before. Enough to pay off her university bills.

After the meal, one of the welders called the well-educated waitress over.

"Ma'am, is this bill right?"

We all stared down at our bills.

"Yes it is, and yes I get asked that a lot." She smiled, hoping we'd appreciate the humour.

"Tell me, can I get a photograph of that university you went too?"

"Why?"

"Because I'd like to have a picture of what I just bought."

She turned sullen. Overly sweet, she waved goodbye, and gave us a parting gift.

"I hope y'all don't get your leg hurt like your friend."

I stopped to challenge her sarcasm but was pushed back into line by a seismic crew bursting through the door.

Tumbling out of the back of a half-ton truck, we gathered on the asphalt in front of a line of red search-and-rescue helicopters. The head pilot motioned to us and we formed a semicircle. He had done this same song-and-dance several times a day and it showed. Around him were several pieces of survival gear. He went over each piece, and I will always remember his last bit of advice.

"The suit you just put on is called an open-water survival suit."

He paused as several people blew on the whistle that was attached to the zipper that went from throat to crotch.

"Don't use the whistle."

"Why not?" One of the loudest whistlers laughed, pausing from puffing the peeper.

"What's the first thing you did when you got off the airplane? You took a piss, right? Every guy that ever used that suit did the same thing. And then they all dribbled onto that whistle. We call them pistols."

It got very quiet, except for the sound of retching.

Chuckling to themselves, the pilots started to load up the Huey. Bag after bag went into the back. Over the preparations for the turbo engine start-up, the co-pilot shouted.

"Which one of you is going to the drill ship?"

I raised my hand, trying to be casual under a ton off suitcases.

"We had a med-evac from there, couple of days ago. Pretty messy."

Our questions were drowned out as the idling helicopter's engine chirped to life. The pilots got very busy and very professional, ignoring us until we were well out over the grey waters. The worker closest to the front leaned towards the co-pilot. There was a brief, intense conversation over the roar of the motor. The welder turned to us and shouted. We all made motions that we couldn't hear him over the whine of the engine. He made a motion with his hands like someone breaking a stick. We nodded. The evacuee had broken his leg. It happens sometimes. The co-pilot motioned again to the welder. There was another intense discussion. The welder looked slowly around to all of us. He made a motion like someone breaking a stick. Then he made a motion of throwing half of it away. Slowly, every head turned and looked at me.

We were crammed in quite nicely. I had this vision of a can of smoked oysters. We all began to sweat. Forget the survival crud they had talked to us about, the only thing we could move were our eyes.

After a half hour of thumping our way north, a set of boats appeared. A tiny drill ship, two tinier supply vessels, and a barge-like icebreaker. They were a matched set, topsides painted white, bottoms painted red. Coming in from a distance they looked like my brother's toys on our green basement floor.

A helicopter is the best way to get a good look at a ship before you arrive. Unless you are surrounded by suitcases and the heads of crewmen flat-nosed to the window. The first sight was machinery on top of pipes, pushed aside by cranes, intertwined with portable containers, all dominated by a drill rig tower. From far enough away it looked like a red and white ice cream cone that had gone *splat* on a sidewalk.

When the helicopter touched down, the first thing I noticed was a thick net stretched over the top of the square helideck. It was there to give traction for the helicopter's skids. It also made it difficult for me to run as I dragged my gear. Inches above my head the spinning blades *thud-thud-thudded*. I sprinted as best I could towards the stairs, aware that beyond the netted deck was the horizontal screen. Beyond that was a seventy-foot drop to the water.

The assembly room looked like a steel baseball dugout. It was just big enough for a helicopter-load of men. New guys gathered their gear in the small room, listening to the first of many instructions from the crew. The instructions were shouted, the words competing with the roar of the departing helicopter, the beep of cranes, and the diesel machinery just outside the scratched Plexiglass. The instructions were short.

"Outside the crew's quarters you always wear this."

I was handed a helmet that didn't fit.

"Get your shit and follow the yellow brick road!"

Obviously enjoying our bewilderment, the supervisor pointed to a yellow painted line which started in the middle of the room, went out the door and down the stairs, disappearing around some machinery.

"Follow the yellow brick road to the purser's office," he repeated. "Who's our welder? The ramrod is waiting for you.

You other mechanics wait here. You're to be transferred as soon as your ships come alongside."

Weighted down with gear, we followed the line through the maze and the jungle of machinery. Under the pipe racks where the miles of drill pipe were stored, under and around the base of the crane, watching not to trip on the wires and pipes that lay across the path. Past the moonpool. New recruits always took a peek over the edge into the splashing waters of the pool. Underneath the hallway, open to the sea, we caught a glimpse of the mini Eiffel Tower that was the drill rig. The crewman who was shepherding us motioned to me and pointed up at the lifeboat hanging from its davits.

"This where it happened. Gawdawful."

As if I knew about what had happened already.

Past the lifeboats we turned a corner and abruptly stopped at the door to the living quarters. We had been gawking and hurrying, so when we came to the sharp turn and stopped we all piled into the person in front of us. Presidents of companies and the lowest oilers had all wiped out on that corner. I once tried to stop a couple of guys from the train wreck but they ended up blaming me for it. From then on I just let them become bowling pins. Lying on your face on a cold steel deck teaches you one important thing—drill rigs have surprises. There are no good surprises on a drill rig.

The ramrod was tall. I looked at him right in the nipples. He was well proportioned and his clothes fit him right. He had a wide-open Scandinavian face with a skiff of blonde hair under his gleaming-white foreman's hardhat. He had used the "work your ass off and wear a red shirt" method of advancement. From the drill floor kelly, which spun the pipe, to the head frame at the very top, he had worked every job on a rig.

For twenty years he had thrown his large body into it. Twenty years of hard physical work with hard physical men. From the heat and flies in the Shah's Iran to the freezing cold in Alaska, he had gradually advanced by blunt, brute strength. Just a nod from him and several hundred men on several ships would move as if their jobs depended on it. Because they did.

"Our job is pretty simple. We make hole." The blonde giant nodded in the direction of the one-hundred-and-eighty-five-foot drill rig.

"Do you hear that? That's the drill working. As long as I can hear that motor bark I know we're making hole. I can pretty much tell how the crew is doing by that sound. I don't like it quiet."

He smiled. I smiled. We stood in the brittle Alaskan sunlight under the orange fibreglass lifeboats on the south side of the drill ship. The north side was in the shadow. Even though it was mid-summer and there wasn't a cloud in the sky, it was beyond chilly in the shadows.

"I need a railing placed there, a frame made for the sign, and a well made for the avgas tank."

The ramrod listed off his priorities. There was no discussion, no pros and cons were weighed. He wanted it done. It would be done. This was his way of getting to know his new employee. Have it done by the end of the week or he'd have the same conversation with a new welder. He was the coach and I was the rookie. He'd get what he wanted. He left me in the stern, gathering up the welding cables. He hadn't said a word about the injured welder.

With my back to the ship I looked south to the beauty of Alaska. In the stern I felt alone with the world. The sun reflected mirrored flashes on the blue ocean. In the misty distance was the north coast of Alaska, which rose to blue snow-capped mountains that cut the sky like an old saw blade.

Alaska. Land of the gold rush, the last American frontier, home of the granite-jawed individual. The country was brittle and beautiful. Easy to love, but hard to live in.

To an outsider there seems to be two types of Alaskans. The first wrap themselves in the Hollywood image of rugged individualism. Dressed in furs and theatre, yelling, "Look at me! Look at me!" This first type has usually lived there for about three and a half weeks.

The rest of the Alaskan people don't act rugged. They quietly, and without flash, endure the winters, with their lips pressed together and their heads down. Their characters are hammered into them by the snow, the trees, the frigid winters, and the all-day sunlight of the summers, with their fogs of black flies. Alaskans are one tough breed. But they are tough in an accepting way. They are a northern people. They don't talk as much as their brothers in the lower forty-eight. They think lots. They have almost a Scandinavian attitude about them. A fatalistic realization that this is the place that life gave them, and that's the way it is. Besides, every once in a while they realize they're living in the skylight of God's cathedral.

BONG.

"Welder to the welding shop! Welder to the welding shop, please!"

BONG.

The ship was six hundred feet long, not very far on a flat city sidewalk. Very far if one has to climb several flights of stairs, leap over pipes, crawl under lifeboats, and skirt around electricians pulling cable from one place to another. Puffing as I climbed the final stairs, I came face to chest with the long, lean ramrod. He stood in the centre of the enclave laughingly referred to as the welding shop. Swallowing my pounding heart, I started to understand why he was lean. His sharp look took in my red-faced, sweaty expression. With just a touch of amusement he barked, "What took you so long?"

"I stopped at a 7-Eleven. What do you want?"

There was a pause as he took this in. Someone had actually snapped back at him. My smiling face hid the biting words so his sharp expression softened.

"C'mon, I need some work done on some stairs."

So it began. Day after day I followed that humourless cyborg along the deck and down the passages of the ship. There was enough repair and replace work for three welders. There were four ships in the flotilla and only one welder. Anyone can be a good welder if he has unlimited time. When the time is short, the quality of finished work separates the journeymen from the hackers. It was a game. A rough, all-out rugby game where I pulled welding cable, cut steel with a torch, ground the structures, and pulled more cable. A game where the opponent was time, and no one could win but someone could lose real bad. The hours melted away. It would seem like I had just started a job and it was quitting time. Start at six and end at six. Bed by nine. Nine-thirty if I was daring. The days flew by. Then the weeks, then the months. Calls home started to boil down to one word: "When?"

BONG.

"Welder to the quarterdeck! Welder to the quarterdeck!"
BONG.

"Hey chief! Whatsa quarterdeck? Iszzit the brother of that Irishman, Paddy O'Deck?"

The ramrod smiled. A glacial smile, but a smile all the same.

"C'mon, I gotta job for ya on the rig."

The jobs blurred one into another. One day I was torching a pipe railing and realized that the welding that I was cutting off looked familiar. A slow realization came over me. It was my welding. It had been there so long it had rust on it. I didn't remember being there on that deck. It was my weld, though. When did I weld it? Was it in the ice of May or with the mosquitoes in July? I stopped and a blanket of exhaustion came over me. A sailor walked by.

"Hey buddy, what's today?"

"Wednesday the second."

"Of what?"

"How long you been up here?"

"Coupla months, I think."

"It's August."

"Three. Three and a half friggin' months."

I stared off to the coast of Alaska. Since that first day I hadn't looked at it for more than a minute. From the most amazing heart-wrenching scenery to now—as attractive as old wallpaper. I was tired, dangerously tired.

BONG.

"Welder to the welding shop! Welder to the welding shop!"

BONG.

"I need a hand. Somebody to stand fire watch. The gas tank is too close."

"I'll see, get started and they'll be along."

I stared at the ramrod. No one was coming. The job would be done by the time a fire watch was posted. This wasn't just a simple railing, it was a fuel tank full of aviation gas. In my mind I saw a leg and some meat, and heard screaming. I was too tired

A helicopter refuels on the base at McKinley Bay.

to play the fool and jolly this guy along anymore.

"I need a fire watch. It's too risky."

It was a statement of fact, not a request. The ramrod turned icy.

"Start the job. If someone's free they'll come and watch."

"I can't start until there's backup," I said to his very large back.

He whirled and exploded. "Do the job or take a window seat!"

"Do you ever hear from Tom?"

At the mention of the injured welder, the ramrod looked like someone had kicked him between his two big toes. He aged ten years in a minute.

"You can't blame me for that. I'm not to blame. These things happen. It was bad luck, that's all."

It was obvious that if no one else blamed the ramrod, he certainly did.

"You and Tom should have had this same conversation we're having now. He should have put his foot down. Now that's all he's ever going to do. I need a fire watch."

There was a very long pause while the giant looked at me. He looked like he was weighing the cost of hiring a new welder. I smiled at him.

"Okay, you'll get your backup."

The space was tight. I was on my hands and knees in the container, one shoulder rubbed up against the gas tank, the other pressed against the steel bulkhead. Holding the tip of the welding rod so that it wouldn't skip out of control, I slowly and carefully struck it on the corner of the steel deck and the tank's outer container. The outer container was designed to hold any spilt gas if the tank ruptured. The smell of fuel wafted into my nostrils. The job had to be done. After our little blowup, the job better be done fast. The ramrod had asked twice about it.

The welding rod melted along the seam. The fingernail-shaped flow was the only thing visible through the absolute blackness of my helmet's visor. I smelled the burning paint, felt the warmth, heard the crackle and hiss of the rod. I was oblivious to the world.

"Hey, get out of there!"

I instinctively flipped my thumb under the face shield and leaned back. I was surrounded by low blue flames. I jumped up as my backup aimed the fire extinguisher at the steel vault that contained the gas tank and the flames. He emptied the container into the well then he grabbed the fire hose and sprayed the whole area with cold seawater. The fire was put out quickly. If the backup hadn't been there this would have been a major incident. That's what they'd call it in the offices of the oil company. I'd call it being turned into a pink mist. After it was all over the young sailor and I looked at each other. I walked over to the phone for the PA system. Giving the sailor a wink, I barked, in my best military voice:

BONG.

"Ramrod to the helideck! Ramrod to the helideck! Now, please!"

BONG.

The two-inch thick hardened steel hull, reinforced by twelve inches of steel ribs, buckled and twisted. The ice carved a four-foot gash in it. Inside the ship, the broken frames stove inwards over the steel hump. It looked like a delicate steel flower that had just opened its razor petals. I had the distinct impression of a Venus flytrap. Guess who was the fly.

North of Alaska, in the Arctic Ocean, the ship Supplier Seven struck an iceberg and started to sink . . .

My knee scrapped over a shattered ship's rib. Sparks shot inside my eyelids as my head hit a twisted pipe. Inches away, water sloshed and gurgled in the bilge. The compartment stunk of oil, diesel fuel, seawater, machinery, and terror. *My* terror.

The ice floe hadn't broken apart like the thousands before it. Untold years of freezing and thawing had made it hard as a diamond. Instead of being shoved aside, it had rolled under the bow of the *Supplier Seven*, giving it a gigantic uppercut with the force of a freight train. The two-inch-thick hardened steel hull, reinforced by twelve inches of steel ribs, buckled and twisted. The ice carved a four-foot gash in it. Inside the ship, the broken frames stove inwards over the steel hump. It looked like a delicate steel flower that had just opened its razor petals. I had the distinct impression of a Venus flytrap. Guess who was the fly?

Right through the hull, from one side of the ship to the other, was a tunnel called the bow thruster. It was six feet in diametre and full of seawater. Inside was a propeller facing sideways. When the ship was close to a dock the propeller would be turned on and the ship could be moved sideways. Underneath the bow thruster was a three-foot-wide, triangular-shaped hole. The crack in the hull was there. That was where I had to go. The space was small enough to be a coffin.

I got into the hole by putting one arm above my head and wriggling sidestroke for ten feet. There, with only enough room for a head, an arm, and a flashlight, was the leak. Oily water snaked down the ship's hull six inches away from my nose. The light's glow was sucked into nothingness by black oil, black water, and black chunks of dirty ice.

All that night divers had worked on the outside of the *Supplier Seven's* hull. Up above, while searchlights slashed the pitch-black night looking for more ice floes, the divers had thrown everything they could into the smashed hull to stop the bleeding. With their mittened fingers they had stuffed hemp rope into the half-inch-wide crack. Then steel wool, taken from every machine shop and kitchen in our tiny fleet, was hammered and chiselled into the crack on top of the rope. Finally, a mixture of silicone and grease was made up and smeared over the rope and steel-wool patch. This made the hull temporarily watertight.

As soon as the lookouts saw an ice floe coming the alarm was sounded and millions of candlepower from the two ships' searchlights triangulated on it. Like London during the Blitz, it looked like we were at war. The light turned the ice a brilliant white in the inky black of the ocean. As the ice drifted closer, the divers were yanked aboard the ship to stand dripping, still connected to their hoses, until it had passed. Then, like human yo-yos, they were hoisted back over the side. They took a terrible beating, slamming up against the side of the ship as it wallowed in the swells.

Slowly, painfully, the sailors, divers, and pumps beat back the ocean. For a day and a night no one slept. Finally, the fire-hose-strength flow of water rushing into the ship was reduced to a black, oily snake of water wriggling down the crack in the hull. How long would the patch stay on? One wrong movement of the ship, one ice floe in an ocean of millions scraping the patch off, and that crack would open its jaws and strike, swallowing anyone still in the compartment. Black, icy water would fill the room in seconds.

It was a welder's version of hell. It was hard enough getting into the hole—it would be impossible to get out quickly. My life now depended on a frantically applied patch of silicone, grease, Brillo pads, and rope. My welder's leather jacket caught on a shard of metal, exposing my naked gut to the burn of the freezing arctic water. For the tenth time that day I cursed my luck to be a ship's welder. I cursed my luck to be *this* ship's welder. I kept on cursing because I was dry-mouthed scared.

A single harsh emergency light bulb swayed with the motion of the ship. A collection of silhouettes standing on the room's steel deck turned out to be the ship's officers.

"Can it be fixed?" asked a voice that I recognized from the PA system.

"Yeah, I think so," I replied with entirely too much conviction.

"Rick, you understand the risks here. If the patch comes off this compartment will flood in a minute. So watch yourself. Whatever Rick wants he gets, okay? I'll be on the bridge. Report every half hour."

After some of the shadows left, the chief engineer kneeled

down and asked in a pure Merseyside accent, "So, whoodeya neeed mite?"

"Some friggin' prayer beads!"

"They're all being used, mite. The crew's been going at 'em in shifts. They all got rope burns from 'em."

The two crew members scraping oil off the compartment walls cracked stiff smiles.

"Shit, was *this* close." Motioning to the compartment, the chief went on, "If we hadn't been down here fixin' the lights and seen the water right off we'd be swimmin' by now."

"I'll tell you what we need in a moment, chief."

Already dreading the trip, I turned back and wriggled over the smashed steel ribs, crawling on my hands and knees under the large bow thruster pipe that hid the damage. Stars shot in my head as it thunked a steel beam. Assessing the damage, I counted the items off on my fingers and yelled back to the chief engineer.

"We need welding cables laid down here, welding rods, the bigger the better, a respirator for everyone in this room, a fan to suck the smoke out, a trouble light, and a loaf of very fresh bread."

"Fresh bread?"

"Fresh bread."

"Raisin?"

"Don't matter."

"Cinnamon buns?"

"Won't work."

"Not bagels?"

"No, it's got to be fresh bread. Very fresh bread."

Muttering to himself, the chief engineer climbed the ladder to the upper decks.

Electric arc welding uses a rod of steel with an electric current passing through it. Where the welding rod ends and the metal meets, one hundred and twenty-five amperes of electric arc should be created. Unless, of course, there's water everywhere. Then it's like standing in a shower and plugging in the hair dryer. Once you and everything around you is wet, electricity will go through your hands, knees, and both top and bottom sets of cheeks. After a half-hour of electrical shocks, the problem was solved by stealing the cook's rubber gloves.

The weld looked just like a miniature undersea lava flow. Slowly, the metal was "flopped" over the crack. Sometimes it worked just fine. Other times hours of work would disappear as the water blasted the new weld to pellets. Jacques Cousteau never watched an underwater event with as much attention.

Outside the night turned to grey morning, morning turned to late afternoon, which turned to black again. The time was counted in welding rods used and inches of crack covered. The chief shouted down over the dead machinery from only twelve feet away.

"Rick! This here's Brian Crow! He's ta make sure ya git outta da hole iffn the patch comes off. We see's your feet so's not to worry, the Crow'll get ya out."

Face down, inches from a pool of oil and water, I shouted a muffled greeting, "Hello sailor, new in port?"

"I see you've been working the waterfront," came the quick reply.

"You must have done something real bad to be down here with me."

"Jeez, just what I need, to spend the next couple of days talking to the ass end of a fat welder bent over a ship's rib. Gives a new meaning to the words 'stout laddie'."

The radio in Crow's hand crackled to life. I couldn't hear it but I knew by the tone it was a question from above.

"Hey welder, the cook wants to know do you need the bread now?"

"Not yet, not yet."

"I don't know what you got planned, but the cook says that his bread is gonna save the ship."

"Just about."

Our baked goods discussion was interrupted by the captain on the radio. "The ship is drifting into another ice pack and the *Explorer Two* wants to move the flotilla away from it. We might encounter some more ice but I'll try to avoid the big ones."

The engines revved up, the gentle rocking stopped, and the ship became a living thing again. Crow brightened considerably. We were moving. The ship was alive. It felt good. It felt good until we hit the first ice floe. The ship shuddered, then hesitated. The welding rod dug into the molten metal puddle. Water from the overloaded bilge rolled up and covered my welder's mask, my throat, my chest. The automatic pumps roared to life, drowning out my choking, spluttering cries. The ship slammed sideways and its broken ribs pressed against my chest and stomach, vibrating angrily. The hiss of several thousand tons of ice dragging along the hull six inches from my head seemed as harmless as the sound of slush in a lake. But if that harmless noise ripped away the silicone patch, water would explode back into my compartment. If Crow was really lucky, he'd get out. I knew I wouldn't.

"Now I lay me down to sleep . . ."

"I hear ya."

"It's the only prayer I can think of."

The captain radioed down for a status report. He told us that it was difficult in the mist to tell the difference between the younger, softer ice floes and the harder multi-year ice. It was difficult to tell until the ship hit it.

Three times we hit multi-year ice. Three times the bilge water rolled up the side of the hull over the welding rod, over my hands, and up to my face. Three times the ship's ribs vibrated angrily against my stomach. The patch of rope, steel wool, and silicone held. Slowly, the uneven hesitation of a ship in ice diminished and a rhythmic swell took over. We were free of the ice pack.

After twenty hours under the machinery, slopping around in oil, smoke, water, and dirty ice, I went back to my cabin for a break. My roommate didn't recognize me.

Four hours later I was back in the coffin. The coiling snake of freezing water was slowly being beaten back. A new danger arose. The oil began to catch fire and thick, acrid smoke billowed up from the weld. Donning a respirator, I heard the reassuring *click, click, click* of the rubber diaphragm as the filters did their job. Crow refused the other respirator.

"I don't need it."

"Oh yes you weeill!"

"How will I be able to eat all this bread the cook keeps sending down?"

One welding rod later, he was asking me how to put the respirator on. Two welding rods and the air became brown. Looking directly at a light bulb, only the pigtail filament was visible. Three welding rods and the smoke was so thick Crow could only get around the compartment by feel. We gave off so much smoke alarm bells rang all over the ship.

Hour after hour, the respirators clicked away. The pile of

spent welding rods grew at the bottom of the bilge. The pace was maddeningly slow. It was a good hour if I sealed a half inch of crack. But slowly, it seemed, the black oozing water was in retreat.

It didn't happen suddenly, but it happened too fast to react. One moment I was welding with the arc under water and bubbling away. The next thing I knew, my face was being pounded by a massive rush of water. The divers' patch had been torn off by an ice floe!

"Patch . . . off!"

"Get out, for God's sake. There's water everywhere!!"

"I'm trying!"

Suddenly, a pair of iron hands grabbed my kicking ankles and I was hauled over the ship's ribs and out from under the machinery. Tools, respirator, welding rods, all were left to the icy water, which shot past us and into the machinery. The pumps that had laid dormant barked to life. Bells and lights went off. Ocean water started to fill the compartment. From above, Crow grabbed my collar and frantically yanked me towards the stairs. The compartment got very crowded very fast. Almost all the crew members appeared at the top. We scrambled up the stairs, falling over sleepy-eyed sailors. The cook, in his white uniform, was first at the door, a loaf of bread in his hand. Angry bells were going off on both our ship and the *Explorer Two*. Shouting the alarm, off-duty sailors ran back to their cabins to get their survival gear. The remaining sailors quickly disconnected all the cables, air hoses, and smoke sucker hoses at the watertight door, which was made ready to be closed at the captain's command.

"Nice that we were out before they sealed off the compartment." Crow's wide eyes and gasps spoke of his fear.

"Wondered about that myself," I said, my voice quivering. "Aw, I owe these guys too much poker money, they can't afford to let me drown."

Twenty minutes later a diver was chiselling more steel wool into the crack. A "shave and a haircut" rap on the hull and the diver was gone. The pumps cleared the water. The excitement over, the bleary-eyed off-duty crew went back to their cabins. Crow and I surveyed the wreckage. Like punch-drunk fighters we listlessly grabbed rags and scrapers and half-heartedly began the cleanup all over again.

After thirty-six hours only the head of the water snake remained. A rosebud-size shard of metal, steel wool, and fibre rope blossomed on the side of the hull. Chiselled into the hole by the divers, what was once a help was now an obstacle. A spray of water from the middle of the rosebud shot across the compartment and hit the bulkhead behind me, spraying my back and neck. There was no way a welding rod would stop that. The divers had done all they could; there was no one else to call on but me.

The two-inch rosebud got my full attention. To weld through it would cause it to disintegrate. The full pressure of the water outside the hull was spraying through the jumble of debris.

"What kinda bread you got up there?"

"Well, we got your basic white, your basic brown, some raisin bread, and six bagels."

"What happened to the doughnuts?"

"I dunno. The crew musta ate 'em."

"What do you mean crew? There's only been the two of us down here."

"I gotta keep my strength up for that long swim. Besides,

you don't need 'em, you gotta body like a mudslide anyway."

"Never mind. Pass me the basic white."

The cook, who without question or comment had baked loaf after loaf of fresh bread, finally got his answer. Taking a six-inch threaded pipe that was much larger than the remaining leak, I formed a doughnut shape with handfuls of warm, fresh dough and lined the inside of the pipe with it. I placed the pipe over the rosebud where the water was shooting out. Holding the pipe over the leak with one hand, I sealed the doughnut of bread inside the pipe by sticking it to the side of the ship with the other. The fresh bread inside the pipe formed a seal. Quickly, because the bread was getting soaked, I welded the now dry pipe to the hull. This completely enclosed the leak inside it. Water started to bubble out of it like a drinking fountain, then sprayed all over the compartment as I threaded a steel cap to its top. With much clanging, grunting, and bruising, the cap was wrenched tight.

Lying across the ribs of the ship, bruises screaming, I watched and waited. Three days had come down to this moment. The smoke and stink of burnt oil and toast dissipated. For the first time since I had begun, the far wall of the chamber was visible. I turned back to the hull. Taking a rag, I wiped down the area one last time. No moisture seeped from the weld.

Slowly, with every bone and muscle protesting, I backed out of the hole. Stars shot as I cracked my head. Same spot. Splayed across the hull, oblivious to the remaining freezing water and bunker oil, I looked up at Crow.

"The leak's stopped. Radio the bridge and tell them."

"Awright! But first I'll get the cook to send us down a tray of those cinnamon buns. I'll tell him we're fixin' the motors."

"I don't want to work with no ski-mo. They don't like me, and I don't like them."

"Maybe they don't like you because you call them ski-mos."

"Well they call us kabloonas, that means fat white walking friggin' whale or stranger or outsider, take your pick. What it really means is white nigger. They don't like us. They don't like us lots."

The crew's resident redneck, discovering he had an audience, continued. "They call themselves Inuit which means the people, so what's that make us? Nobodies?"

"Okay, okay, enough." I put an edge in my voice. I didn't need this crud stirring up my crew. In the whole crew only two of us had spent any time in the Arctic. Twenty men and only one asshole. But this asshole had spent a lot of time nursing his hate. He obviously knew the Inuit, had spent years with them, but didn't understand them. And now he would have to work with one of them.

"Look, we got him. The company's not asking us, they're telling us. Until the job's over, the kid's our responsibility. He'll be treated like any other apprentice."

"How long were you up north?" I asked, looking at the redneck.

"Ten years."

"Ten years. How could you spend that long in a place you hated?"

"I didn't hate it. I just . . ." His voice trailed off. He looked around the lunchroom.

I stared at him. The irony of what he had just said needed space to settle. I looked into the indifferent faces of the crew. The odds were that one or two welders would hate the new kid for what he was, and a couple would fawn over him for the same reason. And the rest? Well, the rest would give him a chance. I looked around the room for any more discussion. Several of the crew just shrugged their shoulders.

"The deal was, the company would hire locals. He's a local. He's starting next week. We'll have him helping you guys on the settling tanks until he gets the hang of it. Al, you take him under your wing and make sure he doesn't kill himself, or one of us."

Al looked at me and defiantly stuck out his chin towards the redneck. I thanked the heavens for old, fearless welders. Al hated the redneck, so the Inuit kid would be safe with him. I shook my head. The Inuit were such a gentle people. Something must have got to this guy. Better keep the kid away from him.

The site was no place for a babe right out of the woods. A nice quiet journeyman edging him into the construction life might have worked. I just didn't want him getting hurt. I didn't want any mother crying over something I could have prevented. I didn't want to see him leave by med-evac. There had been several of those on this project. I didn't want to worry

about someone wandering around, walking under loads, climbing on shaky scaffolding, or falling into acid tanks. I hated the responsibility already.

The day before the last foreman had left on the weekly flight, they called me into the construction trailer. Blueprints on the walls, drafting table full of paper and scribbled notes, the general foreman looked over his glasses, pausing from his telephone conversation.

"We're making you foreman after Jim leaves so get all the information from him today and go get yourself a white hard hat."

Flattered that of over twenty other men I was the one chosen, I began to blurt out a long thank-you with assurances of my eagerness and all that horseshit. He cut me off with a chopping motion.

"Yeah, yeah, well I've seen your crew and the reason we picked you is because Jim tells me you're the only one that's sober."

Jim laughed, the general foreman laughed, I didn't. It was too close to the truth. The boss went back to his telephone. Jim and I were dismissed.

Days later, a half-ton full of native kids showed up. Each kid was parcelled out to the various trades. The leader walked our kid over to our site and introduced him to me. I had socks that were older. His brown eyes were wide, the noise and movement of the construction site pounding his senses. His helmet didn't fit, the gloves were too large, and the boots were new and probably hurt. The kid was shit-scared. I motioned for him to follow me.

"Come here, kid. I got something to show you."

Once we were in the quiet of my new office I held my hands in front of his face and wiggled my fingers.

"See these? I've been working twenty years and I still got them all. Not too many construction workers can say that. Kid, it's not *if* you're going to get hurt, it's *when*. You are going to get into an accident doing this job. It's only a matter of time. Constantly remind yourself of that and you might end up with all of your fingers. Think safety all the time. Think for yourself. If it's dangerous, don't do it. If you get fired on some job somewhere because you refuse to do something danger- ous, you can always get a new job. You can't get a new life. Safety, safety, safety. Always think safety."

Boy, did I ever sound pompous.

"Now, Al is your mate and he'll show you around. He's the old guy out back of the lunchroom. He looks like the Tasmanian Devil. He's got Coke-bottle glasses and a curly grey beard. He's expecting you. Don't get too close though, he's crazy. Yep, last apprentice woke him up from a sound sleep and Al damn near killed him."

I felt good. I had given my first pep talk to my first employee and planted a time bomb. Al would get the kid to watch out for the foreman, which was me. If I ever appeared, the kid would be too frightened to wake him up. He'd go off like a Titan Two rocket. Gawd, I loved the power.

Like most Inuit, he hadn't said a word, but was as obser- vant as an undercover cop with years of training. He came from hunters. He had understood.

I didn't see him for several days as he and Al hid out each morning. I turned a blind eye to Al's slow mornings because he had a bad case of the guilts. He would hide out for the first hours of the day trying to sober up. As the day wore on and the booze wore off, he would work harder and harder. By the end of the day, Al and the kid put out more work than most of the others.

The nicer I was to Al the harder he was on himself. His mother must have shovelled the guilt with a number-nine coal shovel. A simple "How's the job going?" at coffee would make him turn beet red. The kid was the watchdog, but I always knew.

As that winter wore on the newness rubbed off the kid. He became accepted for what he was, quiet and competent in an awkward way. Al would have the kid get equipment and supplies as he slept the booze away in some hole somewhere. Coffee-time was the only time we saw the kid. Al seemed happy with him and so he settled into being just another part of the crew.

One day we got a notice. The general foreman told us to pull the men off the job. Everybody was to be sitting in the lunchroom by two o'clock. They even wanted attendance taken. They were going to X-ray the welds. These weren't your average X-rays; these suckers would blast through buildings. After they were taken, the floor of the building would be speckled with the bodies of birds and mice caught in the beams. These X-rays would rot off very important parts of your body. The first thing I did was find Al in his hole and get him and the kid out of the building. He was disappointed that I knew about his hiding place, and gave the kid an accusing look.

It was April, still winter. It was hot in the lunchroom. We sat, dressed in our heavy welding clothes, for hours. The X-rays weren't going well. We didn't care. After a while, men began to talk.

"Hey Theo (who was born in Israel), how far is Nazareth from Jerusalem?"

"How big's the Jordan River?"

"Ever kissed a camel?"

"Hey Aussie, what are the topless beaches like in Australia?"

"Ever been bitten by a shark?"

"Hey kid, you ski-mos still swap your women?"

Silence. Long, embarrassed, ugly silence. The kid looked at the floor. The rednecks grinned at his discomfort.

I jumped into the conversation to prevent further torture of the youngster. We were twice his age. He was just a kid and we were just a gang of bullies.

"You know, the summer I worked at an Inuit village, the white manager embezzled eighty thousand dollars. The white hydro workers were bringing in the drugs. I had a young kid come up to me and ask me for drugs. When I told him that I didn't sell drugs, he said, 'But you're white aren't you?' Two white guys who worked in the store were smuggling in booze to the twelve-year-old girls, trading for sex. A couple of the weather guys were using the overflow dorms of the radar site to screw the local girls. You know, that was just one summer in only one village."

I was rambling and I knew it. The kid glanced at me and quickly down at the floor.

"They got good reason to hate us white guys."

The redneck looked at the room as if holding court. He puffed himself up a little and started to ramble. I noticed how crooked his front teeth were. His slick grin made me wonder how anyone could ever kiss that filth without being paid. Once a skinny loudmouth, overindulgence and sloth had made him fat. The mouth was the same.

"Eskimo is a Cree word for fat eater or lard eater. That's why the ski-mos want to be called Inuit. The Indians and the ski-mos hate each other. They killed each other off right up until the whites showed up and changed the rules. Ever been to a bar up here? The Indians sit on one side, the ski-mos on the other, and the whites sit in the middle. Kabloona means 'I hate your guts, white man.' When I first came up here it came as a shock that they hated me without even knowing what I was like. I was white and that was enough for them. How much shit can you take before you start fighting back? And then everybody thinks you're an asshole."

He looked up from the floor to the kid, then to Al, then to me. The crew was quiet.

"I don't hate the ski-mos. I like 'em. I like 'em when they keeps up north. I like the older ones." He almost whined. "When they trade their culture for ours a lot of crap starts. They ain't white, they ain't ski-mo, they's all hate."

"Tell 'em, tell 'em," one of the other rednecks egged on.

"About what?" the speaker asked. He knew already.

"About the girl."

"Oh, that."

The redneck moved in his seat like he was settling down to tell a prize-winning story. In a way it was. He waited until the room was quiet.

"Wellll . . ."

He stretched the word out so everybody could gather around, like some politician tapping a microphone and saying "Can everybody hear me back there?"

"I was working up the coast with a drill crew. There was a little girl up there. Pretty little ski-mo. Musta been seventeen, eighteen. She'd hang around and help out the bull cook. Well, things got pretty hot and heavy between us the next couple of months. It was pretty good. I was away from home and getting all the comforts of home too. If you know what I mean."

He winked at the other rednecks, starting a chorus of snickers.

"The end of the job comes and we move on. I says my

goodbyes and leave. That was that. Most normal people woulda thought that. Thanks for the fun, see ya next time. Not her. No friggin' way. Two weeks after I get back to Winnipeg she's knocking at my door. She shows up with her suitcases and everything. My idiot wife lets her in, and she walks right in and sits down in my living room, on my couch. She tells my wife that we love each other and that my wife and kids gotta leave. In your worst nightmare, you can't imagine what went on. She wouldn't leave. I couldn't get her out of the house. The screaming and stuff. Finally, I had to grab her and throw her out. I locked the door. I threw her suitcases outta the window. She stood on my driveway for the longest time, screaming. The neighbours all were lookin' out the doors. Shit, what a mess. Finally a cop car drove by and she left."

A couple of the younger guys chuckled. Anyone with a family shook his head. Some of the men looked at each other, trying to gauge a response. If the redneck was looking for pity, he failed. If he was looking for revulsion, he succeeded. One welder started to chuckle.

"I guess there was no nookie for you for a while, eh?"

A couple of the older welders got up and made exaggerated stretching motions. I looked at my watch.

"Look. It's a quarter to. They haven't finished so let's call it a day and we'll start tomorrow."

The redneck looked around at the audience, surprised that only a couple of the men thought his story was funny. But there was enough of the crew who had laughed to satisfy him. There always is.

There was a general rush for coats and the waiting buses, which were waiting down the road to drive the crew the three miles to their bunkhouses at the camp. They'd be happy that they got to the supper line ahead of every other trade. Tonight I'd be popular. The pounding of their boots on the floor leaving sounded like carpenters let loose in a wood mill.

Al was sitting alone at the back of the lunchroom. The smell of men and the stink of the redneck's story hung heavy in the room. I looked at him. Al challenged me with his eyes.

"You got kids?"

"Three. Three daughters. Yeah, I know what you're thinking."

"Where'd she go? What happened to her? Thousands of miles away from her kin. Walking the friggin' streets of Winnipeg with her suitcases, crying. No wonder she made a stink. She had no place else to go. Are you and I the only ones of this whole friggin' crew who thinks he's a piece of shit?" His voice was a low quiver with a small crack in it.

Al grabbed his coat like it was someone's throat.

"It mighta been worse, Al. She coulda lived with him."

Al snorted as he brushed by me and jumped down the three steps to the gravel below. The welders in the bus started to yell for Al to hurry up. They couldn't hear what we were saying from that distance.

"Al, Al!" I called after him. I stood at the work-shack door, looking down at the old, rough, but good man.

"We only got about a couple of weeks left here, we'll be laying off soon. Some guys are going to be real easy to lay off. Don't start anything or they'll make me get rid of you first."

He smiled and waved his jacket.

"Good idea," he shouted over his shoulder.

Next morning was a beautiful winter's day. Late April and the sun was high and warm. The mosquitoes were still in their eggs and the geese were starting to arrive. The snow crunched under my boots as I walked to the construction site.

I wanted to be there before the buses unloaded the crew. The general foreman, superintendent, and security chief were all in the office when I arrived. They looked up when I walked in.

"Looks like a couple of your guys got into it last night."

"Oh?"

"You musta heard. Christ, it woke half the camp."

"Naw, I sleep with ear plugs in. The only thing that wakes me is when my neighbour starts smokin' up. Who was it?"

As if I didn't know. I just hoped the redneck hadn't killed the old man.

"The guy they call Redneck and that old guy Al. Pretty well beaten up. He'll be leaving today. No charges though. Neither one wants any trouble. All the witnesses said that one brushed up against the other and it just got bigger. They both said that's what happened."

"I'll be sorry to see Al go. He was a pretty good man. Was he hurt bad?"

"Al? Al didn't have a scratch on him. Redneck's going to be spending the next few weeks sucking supper through a straw."

I almost dropped my coffee.

"We got them down at the lockup. They'll be fired and sent home on the ten AM plane."

The whole business was so casual. From the bored tone of the conversation even an outsider could understand that this was a regular event in a construction camp.

"Al's okay?"

"Yep."

I stared into my coffee, thinking hard.

"Look, Al is one of my best men and the redneck's an ass-hole. He's been causing problems on and off the job since day one. If you give them both a urine test right now I'll bet, hell I know, which one will fail. Good riddance. But don't let him take a good man like Al down with him. Al can drink all night and work like a slave all day. I need him. This job's only got a couple of weeks to go anyway. Can't we put the asshole on the morning plane and tell him that Al's going on the afternoon plane so's we can keep them apart?"

We talked for an hour. I wanted Al to stay. He had taken a stand when the rest of us had ignored the injustice done to a little girl. We didn't want to cast the first stone. We didn't want to do anything. We went along. He, in his own crude way, took a stand. I never told the camp officials the real reason I wanted Al. He did what every father of daughters wants to do at least once.

They found a way to separate the two and Al stayed. The crew got witnesses to tell the three camp officials that the poor old man was walking along and minding his own business. They also said that Al was entirely in the right, that most of the damage to Redneck was because he fell on the ice. Several times.

Al came back to work the next day. There were a few questioning glances but most of the crew had seen the fight. He gained brute respect that day. The redneck was gone. Not only fired, he was going to enjoy the wonders of porridge until the wires came out of his jaw.

The crew was in the lunch shack and I sat in the office, alone. I got up slowly and stood at the door. All eyes turned to me. They had heard about my conversation with the general foreman.

"Al, could I talk to you?" Al and the kid stepped forward.

He motioned for the kid to stay. "Watch out Al, he likes you. Watch out for the favour! You better be good to him, Al!"

Al walked in and I slammed the door behind him, for effect. The crew grew quiet in the other room.

"IF YOU EVER DO THAT AGAIN . . ." I went on as long as I thought I could get away with it. Al stood and took it all in. He had heard too. After I was finished, I opened the door. As Al passed through, one of the welders announced in a mock ring announcer's nasal voice:

"Gentlemen, in this cornerrrrr . . . Kid Come By Chance!"

Everybody laughed and cheered. Al smiled.

"Actually, it was Kid Thunderbolt," Al calmly announced. He had fought professionally as a younger man.

"I figured as much."

Three weeks later we stood together in a ragged group, surrounded by our luggage. We looked awkward in our street clothes. The plane was an old one, older than most of the crew. The kid hung around the outskirts of our group. He had come to say goodbye to Al.

Self-conscious as always, he was so shy it was almost painful to watch. He was dressed in a light bomber jacket, baseball cap, blue jeans jammed into rubber boots. By his side was an old .303 rifle with a well-worn wood stock. His suitcase was a doubled-up shopping bag. He had a package of raisins and a bag of flour. Under his arm was a bedroll wrapped in a rubber ground sheet. It was just above freezing. In the ditches and valleys snow still hung in the shadows. The kid started to say goodbye to Al.

"But aren't you coming with us?"

"No, my mom wants me to go back to school in the fall."

"But it's May, what'll you do till then?"

The crew started to wander over to our little group. The kid shrugged, embarrassed by all the attention.

"It's a couple of hundred miles to your home. What'll you do. How will you get home?"

He shrugged.

"You're going out on the land?" Al said. It was more of a statement than a question. They must have talked about this before.

"Yeah."

The crowd grew around the kid. Men started to fire questions at him.

"How many bullets you got for that rifle?"

He held up a half-filled box. "That's all I'll need."

The men looked at each other and back to the kid.

"You're walking home? Cross-country? That's a couple hunnerd miles."

I looked from the kid out across the runway to the vast and stark land of Canada's north. The trees were stunted—the largest ones were chest-high.

"ALL THOSE TRAVELLING TO URANIUM CITY, PRINCE ALBERT, SASKATOON, PLEASE HAVE YOUR BOARDING PASSES READY AND BOARD THE PLANE AT GATE NUMBER . . . ONE."

Gate number one was the door, the only door. The crew grinned. They were going home. They would have smiled at anything.

Al turned to the window. The kid had left the small terminal and was crossing the gravel road towards the tiny trees, towards the land. We handed the boarding passes to the same guy who had booked our flight, taken our tickets, and packed the suitcases onto the plane. Al looked out the window again. The kid had disappeared into the bush. The land had swallowed him.

Staring into the bush, Al smiled wistfully and looked at me. "I asked him about gettin' lost. Know what he said? He said you ain't lost if you don't care where you're going."

He shook his head like he wanted to clear a memory. "Just a kid."

"He'll be all right Al. He grew up doing this Daniel Boone shit."

"Not him, her. She was just a kid. Where'd she go? What'd she do?"

I didn't answer. We both knew.

We stood for a moment and looked out at the land. For the first time since we got there, months ago, we really looked at the land. The trees, tiny cousins of the southern pines, stood out against the pale moss on the ground. Here and there slivers of snow remained in the shadows. The sun, as always, shone sideways across everything. Pity the southerner who has never seen an arctic sun skipping along the earth, gathering all the colours of the prism and turning the land a warm purple.

The grain elevator at Churchill stood out like a beacon
on the shore of Hudson Bay.

On the cold, western shoreline of Hudson Bay a solitary cement grain elevator stands like a giant lighthouse, surveying the icy waters and the vast empty plains that surround it. Near the top of the weathered grey monolith the word CHURCHILL appears in faded paint.

Just to the south, old grey barges are tied to a wharf. In season, they carry goods that the tiny Arctic outposts and family villages depend on to survive the long Arctic winter. At the end of the season they come home to Churchill, battered, beaten, and empty. Well, almost empty.

On the deck of one of the barges stood three men—a foreman and two welders. The old thin welder stood in the bitterly cold morning, trying to look interested. His rheumy eyes stared at a middle distance. Fighting back the urge to retch, he only wanted the dull ache to go away, out of his body, away from his head, away from his life. His stomach flip-flopped. Sticky saliva the thickness of blood filled his mouth.

"Please don't let me shame myself. Not like before. Please." He prayed to himself.

The young foreman stood balancing one foot on the red railing while the other rested on steel angle iron. He informed his crew what the project would be, although it was pretty obvious. After a long moment, the younger welder, straight from the flatlands of the Canadian prairies, muttered to himself.

"A wave did this? A wave?"

Two inches of pipe ran along the top of the barge's railing. Welded to the pipe was steel plating meant to keep the sailors and cargo in and the tops of waves out. A flaw had appeared in the railing the previous season, and the waves had hammered at it until it had given way. Thirteen feet of steel wall lay on its side, level with the deck. The welders looked down at it, the silence underscoring their awe of the power of the water in Hudson Bay.

The foreman looked sharply at the two and broke the quiet.

"Steel is thirty thousand pounds per square inch. Figure out how many square inches of steel are in this bend and you can figure out the power of that wave. You should know that, chief. You taught me. You used to have me figure it out with chalk on a steel tank."

The old man's runny eyes shifted from inside his mind out to the foreman. A look of confusion was focused on the figure in front of him. Then he glanced back to the bent steel.

"Lots."

"Lots." The foreman almost sneered, but caught himself. He was younger and stronger and at the prime of his life. And now he held power over his former boss. But there was a time . . .

The energy between the two men crackled. The foreman gave the older man an appraising look and left. He had crew spread out over three other barges. He was too busy to baby-sit young kids and old drunks.

The older man seemed to sag.

"You okay to work, chief?"

"Used to be my apprentice."

The prairie boy looked at the old man and then to the receding form of the foreman. He turned and started to string welding cables. He knew enough not to ask. The old man stared after the foreman. A shudder racked his body.

In the early morning light the barges looked like just another set of rocks on the beach. They were grey, patched with other shades of grey, and highlighted by streaks of red rust. The weak northern sun caught their scars, their warps and all the damage from the years of hard use. Year in and year out they took a terrific pounding. The barges would bend and sometimes leak but they never failed to put into the tiny ports that lined the northern shores of the bay.

The white condensation of the foreman's breath hung in the air. Even though it was early June, morning frost was common in this land north of warmth. The old man saw the steam and his own apprenticeship flicked in his cotton-filled mind. Another time, another place, another life. Strobe-light visions of a strong young wife, babies with fat little arms whose eyes lit up when he opened the door. It was a time of parties and laughter, lots of laughter. Now the steam locomotives were gone, the company was gone, the family was gone.

The prairie boy clanged large tools onto the barge's thick steel decks, bringing the giant box to life. The older man picked up a coil of wire rope and slung it over his shoulder. He winced. It was a point of pride that he could still put in a full day, whatever his condition. It just seemed that every part of his body now ached from something or other. His left arm was covered in scars. Because he was right-handed, his left arm and leg tended to be under the arc when he welded. Over the years, hot slag regularly found holes in his leather jackets and gave him dime-sized scars. Like badges, he wore the scars from construction sites across the Canadian west. From cities and towns like Moose Jaw, Estevan, Saskatoon, Coronach, Selkirk, Fort McMurray, and Prince George. His nose and sinuses had been re-arranged by the fists of four drunk boilermakers in a Montana border town. As often as not, drunk or sober, he woke most mornings with a dull headache because of it.

For the next few weeks it was the job of the welders to return the barges to a semblance of their original condition. Bent angle iron was to be cut with torches and removed. Replacement shapes from a pallet of new steel were to be cut to fit the gaps and inserted in the holes. Bent steel would be forced back to its original shape. For a time the barges would take on a patchwork appearance as huge squares were cut out of their sides and replaced with red-painted steel.

There was pride in the welders' work. A camaraderie sprang up between the two workers. The old man would fit the steel by running his gloved hands over the gaps. With a hammer ready in his right hand, he would point to a spot with his left. Without a word, the younger man would spark the welding rod where it was indicated and stick the new steel to the old. As the hours went by, the bob-and-weave dance between the men was punctuated with only grunts and the odd one-word sentence.

"There."

The welding went so smoothly that, once painted, you couldn't tell the difference between the old and new steel.

"You know, there's no need to be so careful when you hit the steel not to mark it. Who's to know it's been marked up?"

The younger man gestured to the empty wastes around them. "Besides, the apprentice will be grinding it anyway."

"I'll know."

"That's what I thought you'd say."

Fixing the barge gave the men a sense of saving something, like restoring a vintage car or an old wooden boat. They felt their work had value, purpose. They felt they were putting things right.

A worker came running out from the grain elevator's welding shop, kicking up stones and dust in his wake.

"Didja guys hear that?"

"What?"

The welders gathered around the worker expectantly.

"I was inside working and I heard a god-awful noise that sounded like someone was getting killed and shot all at the same time. So I run outta the shop and there's two seals fighting on an ice floe. They're really going at it. Jeez, whadda noise. A couple of them lady tourists were watching and they got all upset. Listen!" He cocked his ear. "They're still going at it."

Welders from all the barges dropped their tools, hurdled over the sides, and pounded up the gangplank to the dock. They skidded to a stop just in time to miss the fight. The old welder, whose running days were long gone, followed the crowd with a speed that belied his state.

Arriving on the dock, they almost knocked over a couple of spinster schoolteachers from California. The ladies, in their new designer parkas, recoiled from the dusty crowd around them. The prairie boy, aware of the stares, tried to cross the chasm between the two groups by saying to all in earshot. "Wish ta Christ my wife 'n kids were here. Friggin' amazin'."

For the first time that day the old man smiled.

By the time the welders got to the other side of the dock, the champion seal was weaving his head and barking in a victory dance all alone at the top of a small iceberg. The other seal, the loser, was circling in the black water, barking out his defiance.

"That's right, buddy," the young welder yelled. "It was an illegal move anyway! You just slipped! Ah, shaddap. We don't care about what he does to his mother!"

Twenty minutes later the welders, much to the relief of the teachers from the south, dragged themselves away from the dockside like little boys forced back into school after recess. They took up their positions inside the barges, and the noise of metal striking metal slowly resumed.

An hour later a shout went up inside one of the barges.

"Belugas! Lookit the whales."

At the very back of the gangplank, following the galloping crew, a loud voice demanded with indignation, "Hey I'm the foreman, I get to go first!"

"Up yours, you can wait."

"Yeah, for a buck an hour more you can wait."

"Pretty lippy for an old fart."

The old welder smiled to himself. Old Fart was the nickname his apprentice, now boss, had given him a decade ago. He squinted towards the wharf, then quickly glanced towards the foreman's feet beside him, too shy to look his former friend square on.

Spread out at the dock's edge, the workers looked out at the green and black waters of the bay. Here and there, whales spouted and blew, spray and steam erupting and falling. Below the surface white shapes gracefully flowed like a flock of birds.

A smaller baby beluga broke free and darted towards the line of workers standing on the dock, coming closer for a better look. A couple of larger whales shepherded the baby away. The crew stood in quiet awe, watching.

"Didya know that when the first white men came up north the Eskimos tried to describe what we all looked like by calling us Kabloonas, or white whales?"

"Kabloona means stranger." The old man answered.

"Beluga, Kabloona, same, same."

"They thought we looked like that?

"Probably still do."

"Time for a diet."

Despite appearances, the crew was not made up of what you would call hard men. They were just doing a tough job. In construction, the more dangerous the work, the more normal the crew. This crew was mostly family men trying to feed the wife and kids. A couple of them were feeding a wife, and kids, an ex-wife, ex-kids, and the ex-wife's new boyfriend.

"Been in the last barge?" A pipefitter asked his fellow workers over lunch. A couple of heads nodded.

"What's the deal?"

"Just read it next time you're there."

After lunch, several of the crew found an excuse to wander down to the last barge. Although it was broad daylight, inside the darkness blanketed everything. One of the welders dragged in a cable that fed one weak light bulb. Even with that, their eyes had to get accustomed to the scene. The interior was a vast, empty, steel cathedral. Shadows from the light bulb played across the walls. At one time they had been painted white. Holding the light as high as he could, the welder revealed hundreds of scrawled messages. There were drawings, obviously done by small children, and handwriting so shaky it must have been placed there by grandparents. All along the wall, from the floor to the height of an adult, were greetings, plaintive messages, broken hearts calling to one another.

As the barges sailed from village to village up and down the coast, the families would write to each other on the white painted walls of the barges.

"Lookit that," a welder pointed to a shaky scrawl:

> Does anyone know where my daughter is? I love her and miss her. Come home please.

The welders spread out, giving each other plenty of space. In the dim light, they stood reading the words like visitors in a museum.

> To my sons, who I haven't seen in two years, I love you and I'm sorry.

> Hi Rankin! Don't forget me, please.

> . . . is a dirty slimeball.

> Well, at least I don't live in Winnipeg!

> . . . took my daughter, if anyone knows where she is please call.

> . . . please call home. Mom's real sick.

The prairie boy pointed to a wall and in a whispered voice said to his mate, "Makes ya wonder if she called home."

The old welder stared at the wall like he had been struck. He stepped back and looked again. It hadn't changed. Different name, different place, same plea. He didn't smell diesel and salt water anymore. He smelled hospital and death. Wiping his face he hacked and spit.

Please call home, Mom's awful sick.

The urge to hide in a bottle pulled at him. He rocked back on his feet. He had worked hard to hide from that memory. Now it came flooding back. He looked around and found the door. Not daring to look at anything or anyone, he was the first to leave the barge. In the brittle sun of the afternoon, his face shone with tears.

Please call home. Mom's sick.

The rest of the crew left the barge, their welder's boots crunching the gravel on the wharf as they shuffled back to work.

Late that night, several of the men made calls home.

"Hi Kiddo, it's me. No, I don't need no money. Got lots. Been workin up north. Churchill. Never mind that, how's the baby? No, no, there's been no trouble. Remember Tony? He's my foreman now. Yeah, yeah. Well, if you must know, I've been on the wagon quite a while now, quite a while. Heard from your sister? Me neither. Been out to the grave? That's good. I knew you would. Lookit, something happened today. Is that the baby? Good set of lungs on her. Next time I'm in town. Sure, Sure. Lookit . . . I saw something today that reminded me. . . . I started to think about, about . . . yer mother. Mom. I gotta talk to someone. I need to talk to someone or I'll be off the wagon. I started to think about . . . I was thinkin' about . . ."

Then the hard old man, who could make steel twist into anything he wanted, started to quietly weep into the phone.

Steel is made up of tiny molecules laced together to form a whole. Destroy enough molecules and it will begin to tear itself apart. Tearing steel makes a heart-wrenching moan. Failing steel shudders, screams, and cries.

When the repairs were completed, the painters came in and covered the walls with a fresh coat. The barges looked clean and new, untouched and unmoved by the messages concealed within. The grey shoeboxes were ready for another season.

The night sky and the ocean fused into one. It was as if they were on a spaceship, suspended in the cosmic ether of black night, black water, soft sounds. The Milky Way glowed its jagged highway across the night sky. The ship's lights shone as if part of the galaxy. The needles of Kaktovik's lights played across the Arctic Ocean to the south, skipping atop black, brooding swells. The water gurgled alongside the ship's waist. From the southwest came the glow of the refineries around Prudhoe Bay.

They stood by the railing. Although it was still early, the ship's day was done. The two men lounged behind the winch in the enclave where the deck tools were kept. The rumble of the twin stacks of the idling ship sent shockwaves up through their work boots. This was the beautiful time in the Arctic—between the sun going south and the cold catching up. It was dark but still relatively warm. The supply ship idled long, lazy circles around the giant drill ship.

He was far less than half the older one's age. An innocent on his first voyage of manhood. The youth was more comfortable calling the old one "Mister" than his given name. His wide, brown oval eyes shone with innocence. The only whites

A tanker in the fjord at Caper Dyer.

the youth had ever been alone with were his teachers, his minister, and the fat nurse who came to his village twice a month. The man with the briefcase had come to the village and spoken to the elders. They had then spoken to the families. All the boys in school had wanted to go. All his classmates had hired on with the oil company, otherwise his mom wouldn't have let him go.

This was different from the hunting trips out on the land. He looked forward to those times with eager anticipation. The whole village would be on the move, and each day's hunt was a quiet celebration of life. Everyone in the hunt was either a cousin, brother, uncle, or life-long friend. There was laughter, learning, and a chance to show off his rapidly improving hunter's eye. This time was different. This time he was with whites. He was alone.

The older man fidgeted in the presence of the boy. The company had assigned the young Inuit to him. Not used to working with kids, he felt the responsibility keenly. He struggled to remember being that young. Eighteen years old. He was still living at home and the old man was still yelling at him. Now he looked like his old man and yelled at his kids in his old man's voice. Eighteen, that's almost before there was hair. Long-forgotten pink girl skin flickered in his memory. Probably a wrinkled old granny by now. He sucked in his stomach. Eighteen was a lifetime ago. The old one tried to imagine being an Inuit. Scratching his grey-flecked chin stubble, he thought about the open-faced youth beside him. The two of them might as well have come from different planets.

Yesterday, when he stood facing south and said the mountains looked real pretty, the kid was enthusiastic in his agreement. Not like some kids who shrug their shoulders and grunt. Pretty quiet though, not much for small talk. He had those hunter's eyes, that's for sure, always watching. Someone had told him that Inuit learn by watching.

"He don't talk much. Maybe I'll teach him something," the old man thought to himself. Overly conscious of the boy, he pushed away from the railing in an exaggerated manner.

"C'mon. I'll show you how to weld. If you know how to weld you'll never starve."

"Great."

Happy that they now didn't have to make small talk, they

set up at an open spot on the work deck. The old man laid some scrap steel pieces in a tee and started the lesson. His voice was muffled by the welder's helmet. The kid's closeness told him he was watching intently.

"You strike an arc like striking a match. See? Then you let it settle down and keep the rod at a 45-degree angle. Straight in. You're trying to get that yellow puddle of molten steel to look like a fingernail. See? In the shape of a fingernail."

He flipped his helmet up. His voice now clear of the welding helmet, he was almost barking into the boy's ear.

"Now you try. I'll hold the back of your hand so you can get the feel of it. Make those welds straight and don't waver. Think like you're part of the welding machine. Think like your arm's a machine."

They changed positions and the kid tried to strike an arc. The welding rod stuck to the metal. The kid was flustered. It looked so easy when the old man did it. Several sparks later they started again. The kid was a quick learner. By the third welding rod he got the speed right. With the old man's hand gently holding the back of his glove, the resulting weld wasn't half bad.

It felt good to give this to the youngster—something he could always use. Feed a man a fish and he eats for a day. Teach a man to fish and he eats for a lifetime.

An hour later the deck was littered with spent welding rods and the pieces of scrap metal were too hot to use anymore. There was no place left to weld.

"You got pretty good hand-eye coordination. You'd be a natural. All you gotta do is imagine you're a human welding machine and practice and you'll do pretty good. Welding's a good trade. It's a skill you can take anywhere, you don't even have to have pockets."

The kid was rubbing his eyes.

"You got flashed?"

"Yes." He continued to rub his eyes.

"You'll be okay. You can't look right at the arc; it's like looking right at the sun. If you start to get a headache take a couple of aspirin. It'll pass by tomorrow. It's just like sun burning your eyeballs."

"I've been snow-blind."

"Same thing."

"My mom put wet tea bags on my eyes. Couldn't go out in the sun without sunglasses for a long time."

The kid looked up into the blackness that surrounded them, rolling his eyes to test for any damage. Then his gaze hardened as he began watching something. The old one looked to the sky.

"Satellite."

"Where?" The older man squinted. Then, following the youngster's gaze, he located something.

"I see it! No. Yes, dammit, it seems to come and go. These old eyes of mine been welding too long."

"The trick is to find it and then look away from it slightly."

"Yes, I see it now! How come looking away works?"

"I dunno, my uncle taught me that, and he's the best hunter in our village."

The boy paused.

"The weather's going to change."

The older man looked at the youth.

"Looks pretty quiet to me. How can you tell?"

"There's lots of wind up high." The boy's answer was gentle, unassuming. "The stars are shimmering. When it's quiet they don't shimmer much. There's lots of shimmering tonight, it's pretty windy up there. Except the planets, planets don't twinkle."

The welder looked around. There wasn't a breath of wind, not a puff. He looked up in the night sky. The stars twinkled. He knew where Orion was, the North Star, the Big and Little Dippers. Other than that, the night sky was a mystery.

"My grandpa says that the stars are candles, and when the wind comes the candles get blown out. Tomorrow the wind's coming. Stay close to shore on a night like this. My teacher says that the stars twinkle because there's lots of moisture in the atmosphere. But I think Grandpa's right."

"I guess. The only light I get to see at night is the street lights outside my house."

There was a long pause as the two men looked south to the darkened land. After a time the youth breathed deeply.

"Smell those trees. Wow, the air is full of pine."

"Kid, we're ten miles off shore and ninety miles north of the tree line. I don't know what you're sniffing but it's not pine trees."

"No, no. Smell it. You can smell it, I can smell it. The air's full of the smell."

The man scratched his chin. He breathed deeply through his nose. Once, twice, then he began to smile. Faintly but distinctly, he could smell pine. The kid smiled back at him.

"A hundred miles away and you can smell it. Your senses are what mine should be," the old man said with a touch of envy.

He smiled at the kid. In the eyes of the boy he saw the timeless void between hunter and farmer. Between this young man and himself was the chasm of fences and freedom. The kid wasn't going to learn any trade that walled him in. Oh, he might pick up some skill, but his heart would always be wandering the land after the caribou. Other than mild curiosity and politeness, the kid wasn't interested. True wolves can't be domesticated.

The old man tried to imagine the younger's life. How could he provide for his future family in this rapidly changing world? How could he survive? Was it his place to tell the kid that he was looking at a lifetime of disappointment by not conforming? Was it his job to tell the youth that he should stop this hunting foolishness, and this is how you fill out a timecard, dammit? Or should he just let the kid keep some freedom, excitement, joy in his life for however short a period of time. Eighteen, and he's already got what millions of people want and never, ever find.

"Weld long enough kid and it ruins your eyes. Weld long enough and you'll end up being a terrible hunter. But there's one thing you can do."

He handed the kid one of the two push brooms.

"Help me clean up these welding rods."

The Explorer II off the coast of Alaska.
The wave that did it came last in a series of three. The ship that wouldn't move, couldn't move, did. Like a cheap ride at a county fair, the men in the fo'c'sle fell down, then they, the ship, and the anchor chains went up, waaay up.

Six men sat in the fo'c'sle at the very front of the ship. A couple of the sailors leaned against the inclined steel that made up the port-side bow. The coffee was hot and the buns were sweet. The storm jerked the room about. Clothes hanging on nails danced and swayed like a chorus line. The sailors were glad. Heavy weather meant less work now, more work later. And this was now. For several days the storm and blizzard had battered the ship. On the deck above them, four winches, lined up in a row, deadened the fury of the storm.

Each winch, eight feet in diameter, looked like a misplaced hay bale that belonged in some field in Saskatchewan, not bouncing around on a drill ship in an arctic summer storm. The four front winches each held a mile-long anchor chain. At the end of each chain was a massive Bruce anchor. Bruce anchors look like a flippered hand. Pull on that anchor and it only digs itself deeper. There were another four winches, complete with anchor chains and anchors, at the other end of the ship. The winches held their chains in a circular pattern surrounding the ship. The combined anchors held the ship firmly in one spot in the vast ocean. The ship wouldn't move off that spot—it couldn't move.

The rolling swells, their angry foam manes like an endless herd of stallions, battered the ship. The snow and sleet mixed with the foam, painting the side of the drill ship. It didn't roll, or move, or buck, the way ships always do in a storm. It was solid. The eight anchor chains with links the size of a teacher's desk moved and bucked and slashed the waves. The ship's only movement was up and down.

The wave that did it came last in a series of three. The ship that wouldn't move, couldn't move, did. Like a cheap ride at a county fair, the men in the fo'c'sle fell down, then they, the ship, and the anchor chains went up, waaay up. Something mechanical screamed. The tearing sound came from the guts of the ship. The wide-eyed men suddenly had a skylight. The inch-thick steel above their heads began to tear. The deck and hull were ripped and peeled away like a can of sardines. Sailors fell over each other in the cramped space in a vain bid for protection. They looked up from the floor at the disappearing ceiling. Where once a yellow wall with pin-ups, calendars, and coats stood, the men now looked right into the grey-blue teeth of an Arctic Ocean gale. The port-side winch had torn away from its moorings, ripping the steel on the side of the ship. It uncoiled cable as it fell, then disappeared into the frozen rage of the ocean.

 ≋   ≋

"Two sleeps. Only two sleeps more. Then it's home to Winnipeg. Happy kids, soft wife, and safety."

For once it was a bright, sun-soaked day. One of those rare days in the arctic summer that makes a tourist's heart glad. I looked across the deep blue-green of the ocean to the coastline, which underscored the blue slate mountains and their white snow-topped peaks. I absorbed the breathtaking scenery. Like an actor in a passionate love scene with a beautiful starlet, I muttered, "I get paid to do this?"

I was lucky I was far enough offshore that the only thing that could ruin the day, the mosquitoes, were gone. Standing in the bright sunlight was a small group of men. They looked up when I arrived.

"Found a crack in the deck," was the simple explanation.

We brushed off the dirt and the paint from the deck and, on our hands and knees, followed the crack. It was over six feet long and seemed to grow with each swell of the ocean. It started at the corner of the pilothouse and worked its way diagonally along the steel to where the deck and the hull met. Bent over, we looked like a group of young boys, heads down, asses up, looking for all the world like we were playing marbles.

I began to blow the dirt away from the crack. When my head started to whirl from blowing, the mate chipped in. When the captain joined the group and started to blow, the crew got suspicious. They started to edge towards our marble game and the captain shooed them back to work. When we left the area to get equipment to repair the crack, the crew returned. Coming back around the corner dragging welding cable, I stopped to view the collection of upturned bums that greeted me. There must have been five sailors, heads down, asses up, all blowing dirt from the crack.

"Hey guys, Mecca's that way."

"Just lookin'. What's the deal anyway? We got problems?"

"Not now, we got the equipment and the time. The ship's not moving and this'll be fixed in a couple of hours. We have the technology."

I thought of the two more sleeps to go. To stop it from growing we drilled a hole in the deck at the very end of the crack. That would stop the scissors effect. Unless there was terrific tension in the deck, the crack would stop at the hole. We then took an electric air arc and gouged out a "V" in the deck along the length of the crack. This would allow the weld to penetrate the full thickness of the deck, sealing it completely. Once welded it would never come back. That was my story to the crew and I stuck to it.

The discussion at coffee-time revolved around how many more cracks there could be, where they might be, and when they would appear. Hopefully, they would appear two weeks after we left. Our time was getting short. The months had flown by and a crew change was coming soon. Several people in the discussion knew people, or said they knew people, on the *Ocean Ranger*. In 1984, that drilling platform had turned turtle in a storm, taking the lives of all hands. "All hands" meant people just like us.

With the crack came more vigilance and a sense of ownership of the ship's moods. The crack was a symptom. In a storm a minor problem like a crack can become major in seconds. I wandered around in compartments that most of the crew hardly ever used. Usually, a couple of curious crew members puppy-dogged behind. They were convinced that I knew something, that I wasn't telling all I knew. I explained over and over that everything was okay, I just wanted it to stay okay. What I didn't say was that the crack had shaken me. Deep in dank compartments I spend my free time touching, feeling, looking, running my hands over the cold steel.

"What are you mumbling?"

"Nothing."

"You said it's gonna happen. To you? To who? Who does it happen to? Do you know something I don't know?"

"I said it can happen to you. It helps me keep focused."

"Gee thanks. It's good you're friggin' focused. Does that mean we're in trouble?"

"Naw, I just don't like surprises."

This was an old ship. It had had so many modifications to it, so many changes to its structure, I wondered when the straw would break the camel's back and the tired old boat would give out. Just roll over and die. I didn't want to be on it in a full gale. I checked the calendar. Plane day for me was now just one sleep away.

The drill ship would rise and fall with the waves. The drill floor would stay rigidly at one height, level with the horizon. It was separated from the movement of the ship, resting on cantilevers that rolled and bounced with the waves. The cantilevers were like giant teeter-totters, making sure the drill floor and the drill machinery never moved. There were tons of steel rollers under the drilling platform that all moved to make the drill floor stable. The stresses on the ship were tremendous.

The poor, frightened crew that first sailed her in the Second World War would not recognize any part of her now. She'd been widened thirty feet and stripped of any low superstructure. A helideck had been added, a thirty-foot-by-thirty-foot-square hole cut right in the middle for the drill bit, called a moon pool, and a two-hundred-foot tower placed over everything. On both sides of the ship, metal "water wings" or "sponsons" had been added for more stability. Without the extra buoyancy of the sponsons, it would have been in great danger of tipping from the weight and height of the drill tower.

All the places that would be off-limits on a passenger ship were open season for me. I made my way down to the engine room. The sailor there was happy for the company. I explained that I was looking for cracks.

Using the grease gun as a pointer, the oiler indicated the important parts of his life.

"This here's the shaft. There's the propeller at one end out there, and the ship's transmission at the other. Where the shaft meets the hull is called the stuffing box. It lets the shaft turn and keeps the water out."

I stood beside him in the cave-like room. He poured oil into the glass containers that automatically lubricated the bearing on the propeller shaft, which turned slowly, almost lazily. It looked like a smooth forty-five-gallon drum that went on forever. It came out of the tunnel and went into the engine room proper. The walls of the tunnel were covered with rust and pitted by years of dripping condensation running down its face. I looked at the surface and the flakes of rust, trying to gauge the thickness of the metal that was left. I checked the time. It was now only hours before I was to leave.

There were seven diesel motors in the engine room, not the one or two big ones I'd seen in old movies. Seven motors, labelled Sleepy, Dopey, Doc, Grumpy, Sneezy, Bashful, and Happy. Each came complete with pictures of their namesakes painted on their clipboards and engine covers. It sounded a little out of context when one sailor shouted at another: "Hey chief! Dopey's down a couple of quarts!"

"Okay. I'll mark it down. Check Sneezy's compression!"

Five of the massive motors were side-by-side and two were end-on, facing towards the stern. It was a mechanical Stonehenge surrounding a huge dark-grey mound half-buried in the floor of the engine room. That mound was the ship's transmission. All of the horsepower from the dwarves was collected inside it. The raw power was then sent down the silver shaft, past the stuffing box to the propeller.

The noise was a physical force. Standing in the middle of the steel semicircle, the vibration rose up through your feet, making them tingle. It then resonated up your legs to your crotch, making it jingle. Then on into your guts. The noise from the motors would bounce off the ceiling and hit you in your chest, pounding your innards into jelly.

Entering the engine room's control cubical the four-inch door would close behind you and the noise would be cut off like you had just left the ship. You could look out the giant plate-glass window into the backsides of the seven dwarfs and talk in a normal voice. All that remained was a faint hum that seemed to come from everywhere. The engine-room crew would gather in this office, but most of the time they walked around checking the dwarves, wearing huge black earmuffs, like a bunch of scruffy Mouseketeers.

No more sleeps. It was plane day—the happiest day in the rotation. The drill ship's crew was changing. It was with decidedly mixed feelings that I packed to leave. My project was done. The ship was heading out for another location.

A ship riding the waves moves, groans, has moods, behaves, and misbehaves. It becomes a living thing, carrying you in its womb, protecting you from the waves and certain death. Even a ship with an ugly two-hundred-foot drill rig coming out of its middle can give you warmth and comfort. You want your ship to be able to take you to hell and back. You want it to survive anything the sea can hand out. If you fail, it sinks.

We stood in line in our street clothes, surrounded by workers in oil-splashed orange coveralls and red hard hats. We looked as out of place on the deck as if we were wearing pinstriped suits and shiny leather shoes. As I climbed the stairs to the deck in anticipation of the helicopter's landing, I looked out at the horizon. There was a mist and an ominous darkness there. The sailor beside me saw my look and answered my question.

"Low's coming in, weather man says it's a biggie. This old boat's gonna be rockin' for sure."

"Is the storm coming from the Chukchi?"

"Yep. They don't call it the Chukchi Sea for nothing. Going to be a lot of green people here in a couple of days. I'm glad I'll be south by the time it hits."

I looked around at the ship. I had spent months climbing on her, fixing her, nursing her, feeling her, listening to her. I had seen places inside her that few sailors had ever seen. This ship had been the best home I'd had in a long while. I looked up at the rig. Despite all the machines to prevent movement, it swung in a lazy arc.

"I'll be glad to be south too. Damned glad."

ACKNOWLEDGEMENTS

The following stories are expansions from letters I sent home from the Arctic in a long distance attempt to keep tenuous connection alive with my daughters, Rebecca, Tara and Jessica. This book was first written for them.

To Murdina and Dick Brownlee who encouraged and advised at every turn, to Donna and Jim plus their daughter Holly Manser who are my very own cheerleading section, to Betty Ann Watts who took time out to pre-edit, even though she works full time editing her own magazine. To my mother Isabel, the 'keeper of the letters', thanks mom.

To the boilermakers of my local 555, where else can you work hard, make good money, and laugh. To Purvis Navcon, who sent me on the drill-ships, and surprisingly kept me there even after I tried to blow up the place. To Bob Sanderson, Brian Crow, Daryl McLaughlan, Nils Ling, Ross Jopling, John Jeffers, and to all the welders, pipe-fitters, sailors, iron-workers, electricians, carpenters I've ever met, who told me great stories, and then moved on. Cheers.

Finally to my wife Sheila, who gives me enough space to let me make mistakes but keeps me close enough for a hug. You get more beautiful every year.

RICK RANSON, the third child in a family of six children, was raised the son of an enthusiastic, storytelling Royal Canadian Air Force Captain, and grew up in military bases across Canada, from Vancouver to Labrador. A longtime Winnipeg resident, he has hitchhiked from Winnipeg to Mexico, canoed from Winnipeg to New Orleans, driven a camper full of hitchhikers from Winnipeg to Vancouver with an RCMP escort, and lived and worked in Australia. He spent eight years working as a welder in the Canadian Arctic.